the **Clutter**
Connection

Also by Cassandra Aarssen

*Real Life Organizing: Clean and Clutter-Free in 15
Minutes a Day*
*Cluttered Mess to Organized Success: Declutter and
Organize Your Home and Life with over 100 Checklists
and Worksheets*

the **Clutter**
Connection

How Your Personality Type Determines Why You Organize the Way You Do

CASSANDRA AARSSEN

Mango Publishing
CORAL GABLES

 mango

To all those who have felt messy and disorganized their entire lives. I got you.

Table of Contents

Introduction

Have you ever wondered why your children just can't seem to put their toys away "right" or why your husband doesn't put his dirty clothes in the hamper, no matter how often you remind him? Perhaps you yourself struggle with clutter, cleaning habits, or productivity and have resigned yourself to the fact that you are simply "lazy" or just a "messy" person.

Let me assure you, there is no such thing as a naturally "lazy" or "messy" person.

In this book, I will show you the real reason you struggle with clutter and simple solutions to overcome it.

> *Being naturally messy is a myth.*
> *You are not messy,*
> *everyone just organizes differently.*

I am about to take you through a system for decoding your organizational style based on your unique personality. I will introduce you to the four different Clutterbugs, unpack each one in detail, and help you identify which one fits you best. I designed this system through my own journey from cluttered mess to organized success, based on my failure to use traditional organizing methods. I believed, in my heart, that I was a naturally lazy, messy person, and that striving for anything else was pointless. I am going to show you how I overcame my disorganization, just by discovering my true organizing style, and how you can do the exact same thing.

My business, Clutterbug, was born from my own lifelong struggle with clutter and disorganization. What began as my determination to get organized transformed into a blog, then a YouTube channel and, before I knew it, I was working with clients in my community and helping hundreds of thousands of families from all over the world to get organized. It was during this journey that I discovered something that would change *everything* about how we organize our homes.

I had stumbled upon the *clutter connection*. This is a simple truth that is absolutely universal. It is true for both the neat and clutter-free people for whom traditional organizing systems are effective, and the chronically cluttered people for whom organization is a seemingly impossible dream. The clutter connection is simply this: your clutter has *nothing* to do with your actual stuff. It really has *everything* to do with your personality type and how your brain works.

> *"What is necessary to change a person is to change his awareness of himself."*
> —Abraham Maslow

This book, however, is less about how to declutter your home and life and more about discovering and decoding why you struggle with clutter in the first place. The key to success lies in developing self-awareness about your personality and organizational type. Once you understand why you organize the way you do (or why you don't organize at all), you will no longer struggle with clutter and disorganization. You will easily identify organizational styles and strategies that complement your personality, rather than work against it. Knowing and appreciating what makes you unique will help you identify and resolve your clutter issues, from the inside out.

All our lives, we are told how we should organize our homes and, indeed, our entire lives. It is presented to us as a one-size-fits-all program for a "neat and tidy" space to which we are all supposed to be able to easily adhere. Even as children, we are told how to keep our desks, binders, and bedrooms neat and tidy and expected to conform to the one strategy for being clean and organized. When I was a kid, my mom was constantly telling me to clean up my "messy" room, despite the fact that I had sometimes just cleaned it. Clearly, my idea of "clean" did not match hers at all. My desk, binders, and locker were always a disaster at school. Over the years, I had countless teachers tell me that I was disorganized and messy because I couldn't seem to conform to the traditional way of keeping my things straight.

As a result of that constant messaging, from as far back as I can remember, I became conditioned to think of myself as a messy person. Think about your own life for a moment; has your own inability to conform to traditional organizing systems similarly led you to believe that you are a messy person?

The thing about negative thoughts such as these is that they often become self-fulfilling prophecies.

Our thoughts about ourselves shape our entire lives.

When it comes to organization, we've all been shoved into a square box, so to speak, despite the fact that some of us are very round.

It's time to think outside the box when it comes to organization!

It's time to stop trying to fix what doesn't work and focus instead on what does!

I'm going to show you that, by simply knowing your organizing personality type, you will become happier, more organized, and much more productive. We are going to discover and identify your clutter connection.

Disclaimer: This book isn't going to be the usual self-help book. I'm not going to pretend that I have some magic solution that will transform your life overnight, and I'm certainly not going to pretend that I have my own life together. I'm a total hot mess, but I'm an *organized* hot mess.

Here is my *other* disclaimer: I'm not going to tell you how to organize your home. I've never even seen your home—how could I possibly know how to organize it? You see, that is exactly the issue that you have been facing up until now. **You have tried to organize your home and life based on *other* people's and the general expectations of what organization "should" look like.**

Organizing isn't one-size-fits-all.

Here *is* what this book is going to do for you: **It will give you amazing insights into your own strengths and abilities.** This book will hold a mirror up to your personality and give you the gift of self-awareness. I'm going to be your own personal cheerleader, showing you all the things that make you the amazing, organized, and productive person that you are (even if you don't yet believe it yourself). You are going to become an expert in organizational systems that work for you and your family. You are going to be a full-blown badass organizing *boss*.

I will give you some hints, tips, and tricks that I have learned along my journey to get you started, and then I will leave you to your newly discovered genius. You will amaze yourself with how fast your level of organizational mastery unfolds, once you know where and how to begin.

This journey is not going to be easy, but I guarantee it will be worth it. You probably have some bad habits that will need to be addressed and changed, but I will walk you through the process and make it as easy and painless as possible. You will have bad days, heck, you will have bad *weeks*. You won't always do your dishes every night and sometimes your laundry will pile up. That's just life. **But this is my promise to you: this book will give you the tools, knowledge, and confidence to get back on track during those bad times.**

Soon, you will feel in control more than you feel out of control. Your life *will* get easier. Making life easier is what organization is all about. It's about simplifying and streamlining your daily life so you can be more productive, have more time, and, most importantly, feel less stress and more happiness. I'm not just talking about organizing your home; this is about organizing your entire life, and it's much easier to do than you think.

How do I know this? I have been where you are. I would even bet that I was messier and more disorganized than you are now. I lived with actual paths carved into waist-high piles of clothing and trash from my door to my fridge, bathroom, and bed. Even when I attempted to control the chaos, my closets, drawers, and every other hidden space were stuffed so full, I could never find anything. I spent the majority of my life feeling messy, disorganized, frazzled, and like a total failure. I was always late, always broke, and always overwhelmed.

So what changed? How did I transform from Super Slob to Organizing Expert? How did I go from a stay-at-home mom with ADHD, living in a completely disorganized home, to someone running a successful organizing business helping over half a million people from all across the world? ***I stopped copying other people.*** I stopped trying to emulate systems and solutions that I saw on television or in magazines. I stopped trying to plan and organize my life the way I saw my friends and family members doing it. Instead of trying to replicate other people's systems, **I discovered the systems that work best for me and my personality type.** I stopped beating myself up over my failure to adapt to the *idea* of what an organized and productive life looked like, and instead worked with my strengths to create an organized and productive life unique to me.

My home isn't perfect, and I am absolutely not perfect either. The idea that everything needed to be perfect was *exactly* my problem in the first place. I'm embracing my "good enough" self, and guess what? My home is always clean and clutter-free, and I spend less time cleaning and organizing than I ever did before. My business is thriving. I am insanely productive, and I can honestly say that I *love* my life. I feel *in control*, and that is something that I never thought would happen for me. It is such a great and liberating feeling, I want the same for you.

If you gain nothing else from this book, I want you to leave understanding this one simple truth: you are incredible just the way you are. I am going to show you how you can have an organized and clutter-free home, without having to compromise or change one single thing about your personality.

If you are struggling to get your life together, drowning in clutter, or you feel as though you are lacking basic organizational skills, I want you to start by giving yourself a break. I want you to be open to the possibility that *none* of those negative statements are true and the real reason that you have failed up until now is that you have been trying solutions that are designed for someone else's personality. **Albert Einstein once said, "If you judge a fish by its ability to climb a tree, it will live its life believing that it is stupid." You are that fish, my friend, and traditional organization is the tree. There *is* another way and there *are* other options.**

At the end of this book, your home will not look like mine. Heck, I hope your home doesn't look like *anyone* else's. Your space will be a unique creation that *you* have designed, filled with the things you and your family love and cherish. It is organized in a way that works for your and your family's unique styles.

So, my perfectly imperfect friend, let's jump in and discover your unique organizing style and how you can work with your natural style to design the life you've always dreamed of.

Before we dive in headfirst, repeat after me: "I am a hardworking, productive, and organized person." Heck yeah, you are! Say it again! "I am a hardworking, productive, and organized person." Now let me show you how this is so incredibly true, even if you don't yet believe it yourself.

Chapter 1

The Messy Myth

I'll never forget the day I discovered I was not, in fact, some sort of organizing genius. After years of struggling with my own clutter and mess, I had *finally* stumbled upon a system I could actually use *and* maintain long-term. Gone were the traditional detailed and micro-organized solutions I had tried so hard to emulate from television shows and various Pinterest posts. After years of feeling guilt and shame for not being able to use these complex systems, I realized that my brain just didn't work that way. My brain is full-on ADHD, and I don't have the patience or the self-discipline to open a lid or find the right compartment when putting things away. As soon as I'm done using something, my brain has already moved on to the next thing, so putting stuff away properly is always the last thing on my mind. I need easy solutions that take zero thought and even less effort to maintain. This ADHD girl needs *fast and simple* organization.

I joyfully donated the dozens of pretty matching bento-box-style containers that just never worked for me, and I even gave away that crazy expensive paper filing system I had ordered online. In their place were pretty open baskets, complete with simple labels, allowing me to literally toss my things back into their home when I was done using them. I was totally convinced that I had discovered the Holy Grail of organizing solutions. **Being *less* organized was actually making me *more* organized.** It sounds insane, but shifting my perspective of how an organized space was *supposed* to look actually made me a more organized person.

It was this new perspective that convinced me I was some sort of an organizing *super genius*. I started sharing my newfound wisdom with anyone who would listen. I would enthusiastically claim that *most* organizing systems were just way too complicated, and even though they were great in theory, the average person just couldn't...or *wouldn't* keep them up long-term. I honestly believed that *most* people fell into the same category as me, despite the fact that almost *every* solution seen in magazines, on television, or in stores was tailored toward a more detailed sort of organizer.

The truth was, my husband had no issues using traditional detailed systems and thought my new simple systems were a little half-baked. I thought that was his total perfectionist talking, and I dismissed his objections out of hand. Surely that was the opinion of the *few*, not the *many*. When I shared my new lazy system with my messy friends and family, I was super excited to learn that they all felt the same way, and the *simple* approach was now working for them too. I was completely enamored with my new perspective and insight on clutter. **The *majority* of organizing systems were created solely for the personality type of the *minority* of the population!**

My lifelong struggle with being messy finally made sense. Truth be told, I thought I was really onto something. I was convinced that the whole world was trying to force themselves into one organizational style, when in fact, there was more than one way to organize. My "stick it to the man" approach to life was finally paying off and, high on fumes from dollar store plastic containers and chalkboard labels, I launched my own organizing business with the enthusiastic intent of blessing the world with my newfound expertise and wisdom. To my delight, my "less is more" approach to organization was actually a huge hit...for a while.

All good things come to an end I guess.

Fast forward one year, and I'm standing in a client's home office as she sheepishly explains that the paper system I designed for her "just isn't working." I held in my tears (and thankfully resisted the urge to throat-punch her), as this was the *THIRD* time in as many weeks that I'd come back to redesign her space. Did I mention that my redesigns were all pro bono? *Yeah*, in my organizing arrogance, I had declared to all of my clients that, if they were not 100 percent satisfied, I would redesign the space for free until they were. I was now *seriously* regretting that promise.

Walking into that third visit, I believed that this client was just simply lazy. The first system I created for her huge piles of paperwork was a simple basket system, similar to the one I used in my own home. One basket for bills, one for receipts, one for current clients, and so on. No extra micro-sorting into small categories such as "Electricity" and "Gas," just one macro-organized pile of mixed-up "Bills" in a pretty basket. Her reaction to my "genius" simple organizing solution was less than enthusiastic.

"Nothing is even really organized," she gasped in horror as she surveyed the rows of pretty matching baskets labeled with simple categories such as "Home," "Manuals," and "Taxes." She insisted that she couldn't find anything at all and that it was in fact, less organized than the mountains of paper piles that she had started with. I assured her that this system had worked for all of my previous clients and that she needed to simply "get used to it." A week later, she informed me that she would never get used to it and that she needed a much more detailed system. She craved order and perfection. I was completely shocked. Order and perfection were not my friends. Apparently, not everyone was made for my simple and easy organizing system after all.

Her redesign used filing cabinets instead. I made her a traditional filing system, complete with color-coding for all the hundreds of detailed categories and adorable tiny labels for her hoard of papers. I sorted...for days...and created a very orderly and traditionally perfect paper filing system. I even made her a little printout directory and quick-find guide for her files. I thought it was overkill, but she was thrilled. She was a perfectionist, through and through, and I had created a "perfect" organizing system for her paperwork.

I left her home resigned to the fact that some people really *do* love the traditional organizing systems and, therefore, there must be *two* different ways to organize a space; simple or detailed. These two systems were completely dependent on the person's personality. Traditional "type A" personalities (competitive, *highly organized*, ambitious, perfectionist) needed traditionally detailed systems, while "type B" personalities (such as myself) needed a more laid-back and easy-to-use organizing solution.

One week later, I was back in her office for a *third* redesign because she couldn't, and I quote, "put anything away" with the new system. She had pulled dozens of file folders out of the filing cabinets and spread them out on every surface, including her desk, the sofa, and even the floor. Embarrassment flushed her face as she scanned her messy office and whispered, "This just works best for me, I need to *see* my papers. I can't bear to put them in the filing cabinets, I'll forget I even have them. I'm just a messy person, I guess. Maybe I'm just too lazy to ever be organized."

This is when realization hit me like a freight train to the face. She wasn't *lazy* or *messy*. This incredible woman standing before me was the opposite of lazy in every way. She had her master's degree, her law degree, and had even recently opened her own law firm. She loved to cook, sew, and paint in her spare time. Laziness and disorganization were *not* the reasons her office was drowning in paper clutter. She was not messy, she just organized differently.

I should have realized the difference earlier because, in my own battle with clutter, I had also resigned myself to the idea that I was just a naturally messy person. I had spent the first twenty-eight years of my life believing the lie that I was just not good at cleaning and organizing. In fact, the perception I had of myself as a lazy and unproductive person was so deeply rooted, I always assumed I would fail even before I began a new task. Despite my willingness to change and many attempts to do so, I never really believed it would happen because I had failed so many times in the past.

I had set up a traditional paper filing cabinet in my home, but I just couldn't seem to find the motivation to put paper back into its appointed category. Mail would come in the door and never make it into the elaborate sorting system my husband had set up. I had organized my bathroom closet with matching stacked plastic containers, carefully sorting my products into micro categories such as "Pain Relievers," "Allergy," "Stomach," and "Bandages." The truth was, no matter how much I wanted to, I would never take the time to put things away in their proper container when I was done. I simply set the items beside or on top of it, resulting in a messy closet in no time flat.

It wasn't until I stopped trying to conform to the "traditional" sorted category and micro-organizing style that I finally stopped the madness of endlessly tidying and re-tidying my home. I stopped looking at what I couldn't keep clean and tidy, and started looking at the spaces I could. Once those spaces were identified, I asked myself one simple question...why?

I could easily put the pain reliever bottle away when I could toss it into a large bin labeled "Medicine" along with all the other bottles of pills. Clean laundry stopped living in laundry baskets on the floor and started getting tossed into open bins labeled "Pants" and "Pajamas" in my closet. Toys, makeup, office supplies, and even food could be chucked from across the room back into the appropriate bin, making putting things away beyond fast and easy. For me, a simple, less-sorted, less-organized system was the secret to success. When I replicated this simple system in every closet, drawer, and storage area throughout my home, I no longer struggled with chaos and clutter. Everything just started finding its way home, *like magic*. I still struggle with that voice in my head telling me that I'm a hot mess. I certainly don't organize and clean my home in the traditional sense, but it is clean and organized nonetheless.

When it came to my fabulous yet frustrating lawyer client with the serious paper addiction, I was trying to shove her into the "traditional hidden organization" box. Let's face it, not only are most organizing solutions detailed, but they also typically involve putting your belongings "away" and "out of sight." I had never even considered organizing another way. It was at that moment, while staring at her piles of paper clutter covering every surface, that I again asked myself that one simple question...why? Why do these papers all spread out on the floor work better for her brain than stored in the filing cabinet? The answer: She was a visual organizer.

Instead of hiding her paper in filing cabinets or baskets in her closet, I filled an entire wall in her office with vertical paper-filing racks from floor to ceiling. These magazine-rack-style organizers held her sorted and color-coded file folders. Instead of being spread out on her desk and floor, they were visually spread out on her wall. We also installed bulletin boards and memo boards above her desk for important reminders and inspirational quotes. I finished it off with a pegboard to hang her daily-use office supplies.

In the end, almost every inch of her office walls was filled with something: art, inspirational quotes, and visual organizing solutions. It was definitely not my ideal organizing setup; in fact, I found myself anxious, distracted, and completely overwhelmed in the space. But this wasn't my space; it was hers. Instead of feeling anxious and overwhelmed, her bright and full office made her feel focused, inspired, and energized. We were complete polar opposites in our organizing personalities.

We returned the filing cabinets, and she sold all the "hidden storage" units in her office, opting for open bookcases instead. She had fully embraced her visual organizing style and beamed as she gushed to me about her plans to replace the upper cabinets in her kitchen with open shelving. She finally knew herself, really knew herself, and realized that she wasn't a messy person at all. She was a visual person, and she needed to organize accordingly. It was as though a weight was lifted off her. I was overcome with emotion as I watched her look at her home, and herself, in a whole new light.

I saw her in a new light as well. This was the lightbulb moment that changed everything about my career as a professional organizer. I realized that organizing isn't one-size-fits-all. What works for one person most certainly doesn't work for everyone. Organizing systems need to be as unique as the person and the family that use them. Each space has to be designed based on their unique organizing styles in order for it to stay clean and organized. It was this new organizing philosophy that transformed how I organized my own home and my clients' homes, and has helped hundreds of thousands of people from all over the world finally get organized for good.

As my professional organizing business grew and I began helping *thousands* of families from all over the world, I was determined to research, identify, and categorize all the different organizing styles that I was seeing in so many people's homes. After years of practice, I could *instantly* know someone's style by stepping into his or her space, or even just by *speaking* with him or her for a few minutes about clutter issues. I was an expert at the different styles, and I had even narrowed it down to **four distinct personality types**, but I struggled to articulate these types in a way that was simple and easy to understand.

I created an online test to help people identify their style, but even the test wasn't always accurate. I just couldn't find a way to take what I had learned inside my head—and what I had come to instinctively "know"—and say it in an easy and concise way.

It was during an interview with a local radio station that I had my eureka moment. It all came down to two simple words: **abundance and simplicity.**

When asked about the different organizing personality types, I was struggling to find the words to describe a person who craved visual organizing solutions. So many people want to actually *see* their stuff, and I was totally blanking on finding a positive way to describe this. Visual personality types feel anxiety with traditional minimally organized spaces, just like some people feel anxiety in a space that has a lot of visual distractions. My explanation of the differences was usually long-winded and confusing, but during this interview...it hit me... the opposite of minimal is *abundant*. About half the population craves *visual abundance* in their homes, and I finally had an easy and positive way to describe it!

So "abundance" was the winning word, but I was also using the word "minimal" in describing the personality types that prefer to have their items organized out of sight. The problem with this word was that it was now associated with the "minimalism" movement, and, while half the population craves *minimal* visual distractions in their homes, they were not in fact, *minimalists*. Instead, I settled on the word *simplicity*. **Visual simplicity versus visual abundance.**

I can use the words simplicity and abundance to describe the other side of these four personality types as well. There are two very different ways to organize your belongings: micro-organizing versus macro-organizing. Micro-organization is all about having detailed, subdivided categories, with accuracy and functionality being the main goal. Macro-organization has broader, simpler categories, with ease of use being the top priority. People who prefer micro-organizing, with a more detailed and subcategorized system, crave **organizational abundance**. Those who prefer a macro-organizing approach need fast and simple solutions, or **organizational simplicity**.

Do these personality types overlap? Of course, but I can *promise* that you fit into one category more than any other and, once you identify and understand your organizing personality type, everything will change.

Now that I had this language to describe the four personalities, I gave each one an appropriate bug title, and thus the Clutterbug Classification System was born.

The four categories are as follows:

- **Ladybug** – Craves Visual Simplicity with Organizational Simplicity

- **Cricket** – Craves Visual Simplicity with Organizational Abundance

- **Bee** – Craves Visual Abundance with Organizational Abundance

- **Butterfly** – Craves Visual Abundance with Organizational Simplicity

It's that simple: the entire human race sorted into four categories based on how they like their belongings cared for and displayed.

You can easily identify your own personal organizing style by taking a look at a space in your home or at work that just seems to *stay* clean and organized. Maybe it's a desk drawer or the bookcase in your living room. Perhaps it's a filing cabinet or your daily planner. Ask yourself, is this space visual or hidden? Do you prefer to see your belongings or have them out of sight? Is this space using a micro (lots of smaller categories) or macro (a few larger categories) organizing solution?

It's such a simple concept that it has gone unnoticed until now. Instead of trying (and failing) to make your home and your life fit into a certain mold, it's time to create your own. **You finally can have the answers to the questions that no one has ever thought to ask: "*Why* does my home look the way it does and *what* is the *meaning* behind my mess?"**

In the next chapter, we will dig deep into the four different organizing personality types and identify your style, and then you will finally be able to understand yourself in a way that you never have before.

So, repeat after me:

"I am not messy. I am an organized and productive person."

Now, let me show you how you can prove this to yourself.

Chapter 2

What Clutterbug Are You?

Butterfly

VISUAL
ABUNDANCE
·
ORGANIZATIONAL
SIMPLICITY

Bee

VISUAL
ABUNDANCE
·
ORGANIZATIONAL
ABUNDANCE

Ladybug

VISUAL
SIMPLICITY
·
ORGANIZATIONAL
SIMPLICITY

VISUAL
SIMPLICITY
·
ORGANIZATIONAL
ABUNDANCE

 **Cricket**

The Science Behind the Clutterbug Philosophy

Before we jump right into the organizing personality test, I first want to share with you some of the "science" behind the different organizing styles and how I developed it.

Disclaimer: There is actually no defined science involved (*yet*).

However, I've spent years observing my family, friends, and clients, trying to link the different organizing types to other personality traits or to one's particular upbringing or even family history. I wanted to more deeply understand why some people are visual organizers while others are not. Why is it so easy for one person to use a detailed filing system every day, while others just make a pile? Surely I thought, there must be an easy way to wrap this whole concept up with a neat and tidy bow. Unfortunately, the more I dug into the underlying explanation for why some people organize differently from others, the further I actually got from an easy answer. Turns out people and psychological profiles are complex!

While there are shared characteristics that apply broadly to people in each of the categories I've defined, these characteristics certainly do not apply to *everyone* in the group in every given situation. So don't worry if you were already thinking, "I'm a Cricket, but my house looks more like I am a Ladybug." Like a lot of things in life, there is a spectrum to the Clutterbug system. During the ups and down of its development, I found there are also a lot of personality traits that I expected to fit neatly into specific organizing categories but, in the real world, just don't. **Despite having an anti-analytical brain, I still wanted to create**

a test and system that provided concrete, indisputable facts and figures for analysis! However, in the end, while there are certainly four distinct organizing types (and tens of thousands of people now validating this theory with real results), a list of personality-based similarities within those types (apart from organization) just isn't easily defined. Therefore, it is important to understand as we delve into it that, without having a clear and concise list of personality traits for each organizing personality type, it is hard to create a test that is going to be 100 percent accurate, so consider yourself warned.

Is Organizational Style Related to Learning Styles?

This first question I wrestled with is a good one, isn't it? At first, I was certain there was a correlation between the different *organizing* styles and the different *learning* styles. There are many different ways to learn new information, and for the basis of my Clutterbug research and development, I used the VAK learning style models developed by psychologists in the 1920s. This model is still recognized as the one of the three main learning style models today.

What Is the VAK Learning Styles Model?

According to many psychology and education professionals, most of us learn best in one of three ways: **visual, auditory, or kinesthetic**.

Visual

A visual learner absorbs
and retains information
better when it is presented
in pictures, diagrams,
and charts.

Auditory

An auditory learner prefers
listening to information and
responds best to lectures, group
discussions, or tutorials. Recording
his own voice and playing it
back during studying
is also effective.

Kinesthetic

A kinesthetic learner prefers a
physical experience. She likes a
"hands-on" approach and responds
well to being able to touch or feel
an object, or prefers to "figure it
out" rather than being taught
by someone else.

In early versions of my Clutterbug test, using VAK, I theorized
visual learners would also be *visual organizers*, since visual
individuals learn best from looking at pictures or graphs when
processing new information. By the same token, audio learners,
who learn best from listening to others speak rather than reading
written instructions, should prefer a more *minimal* living space.
While this sounds as though it would make a lot of sense, and
many visual organizers *are* in fact visual learners, and many
audio learners in my life *do* crave visual simplicity, the truth is,
these assumptions can be misleading.

**In fact, the biggest monkey wrench tossed into the gears of
the first draft of my wonderful theory was *me*.** I *crave* visual
simplicity, but I'm totally and 100 percent a visual learner. I
wanted so badly for there to be a connection to learning styles,

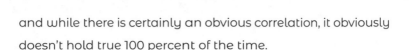

and while there is certainly an obvious correlation, it obviously doesn't hold true 100 percent of the time.

Left Brain versus Right Brain

When I think of a visual person, I imagine someone who craves bright colors and bold home decor. On the other hand, when I think of a person who craves simplicity, I imagine someone who loves a simple and muted color scheme. Therefore, in the early stages of developing the system, I also foolishly assumed there was a connection between a person's organizing style and their creative tendencies.

It's easy to assume that those who crave visual abundance must be more creative and artistic than those who need visual simplicity. While this may be true in many situations, it certainly isn't true in *all* of them. The opposite assumption could also be made: Those who crave visual simplicity are not as creative or artistic as visual organizers. Again, this is most definitely not the case. Take myself, for example. I need visual simplicity in my home, but I love to craft and create and consider myself a very artistic person. I also know many visual organizers who don't have a creative bone in their body.

Nature versus Nurture

"Nature versus nurture" is also an area that I needed to consider. Does it play a role in the drastically divergent ways that people organize and maintain their homes? Were people born with a certain organizing brain type, or was it a learned behavior, influenced by our parents' organizing style?

I see connections to both. Almost all the hoarders I've worked with have come from families with hoarding tendencies. One could argue that this, in fact, is proof of it being a *learned* behavior. But what if the tendency to become emotionally attached to our belongings has a hereditary component instead? How do we explain the fact that so many children who come from neat, organized families later struggle as adults to be neat and organized themselves? Can we simply blame bad parenting? If that is the case, why do children within the same family often grow up to have different organizing styles, despite being raised the same way? These thoughts only drove me back to an earlier theory that it must have a direct connection to a person's innate personality type.

The one idea, which I now hoped would always prove true (and has consistently been my experience with many clients), is that the logical and analytical brain types almost *always* prefer detailed and categorized organizing systems.

I held onto this one last personality-trait theory for dear life, but I have recently met some analytical thinkers who just can't maintain a detailed organizational system and require a simple one instead. Perhaps reading about my trials and errors in this book will entice a PhD candidate somewhere to research and collaborate on this further, but until then I am only left with...

The Logical Conclusion

You can't judge a person's organizing style by personality alone. While there are definitely certain traits that the majority of people in each category share, it is not always 100 percent accurate.

So, how *can* we identify a person's organizing personality style? The best way to discover your organizing type is to, just as I did, take a look at the systems that *are* working for you. Are you able to keep your files organized at work? Are you always able to find your keys when they are on a hook? Do you use your phone to track your appointments or do you prefer a daily planner or calendar hung on the wall? The answer is quite literally staring you in the face every day (or hidden in a drawer). You just need to take a look around to really see yourself in a whole new light.

And remember: Not everyone organizes the same way. Just because a system has worked for one person, that does not mean that it will work for everyone. While the *why* is open for debate, I have mastered the *how*. **I have testimonials from clients and my global online community who have transformed their lives and their homes just by discovering their Clutterbug organizing style.** I have seen the immediate effect that identifying your style can have on, not only your space, but your self-esteem and your self-worth. **You are not messy, everyone just organizes differently.**

Every day, I receive hundreds of emails from people who have felt and seen the immediate impact of knowing themselves through the Clutterbug system. Now, I will help you too. Let's identify your unique style and work from your strengths to help you become more productive and lead a much happier life.

Let's Get Organized!

Repeat after me: "I am a hardworking, productive, and organized person."

Heck yeah, you are! *Say it again*!

"I am a hardworking, productive, and organized person."

Now, let go of those traditional perceptions of what your home is supposed to look like. Let go of how you *think* you are supposed to organize and plan your life. Let's stop looking to others for inspiration, and instead take a step outside the "traditional basket" and look inside ourselves for the answers. Every time we experience a little bit more self-awareness, we are also experiencing self-growth. **That is what this book is all about: knowing yourself better so that you can gain the self-confidence required to run your home, office, and life like a boss.**

Is discovering your style going to transform your house overnight? Of course not. Here's what is going to happen: You are going to give yourself some much-needed grace. You are going to stop telling yourself that you are messy, lazy, or unproductive; those are the lies that have been weighing you down and creating roadblocks in your life. **You are going to see yourself—and your home—for what you really are: unique and amazing**. No more wishing for something different or feeling bad for the way things are now. Knowing yourself means appreciating yourself, and appreciating all that you have, as well. It's going to be hard. It is going to require that you roll up your sleeves, turn off the television, and make things happen for yourself. No more excuses. No more lies. No more self-hatred. This journey WILL be challenging, but it will also be worth it.

For years, I aspired to become a more detailed and "traditionally organized" person. Fantasy Cas is going to organize her computer into neat and logical file folders one day. She is going to make time to redesign her filing system so that her folders are subdivided into micro-organized categories, which are filled with files saved by *both* name *and* date for easy finding. Real-life Cas has a desktop so filled with crap that she can't see her background and has only one folder, called "desktop rando stuff," where she drags and drops all her unnamed and undated files when her desktop gets too full. How do I find my important files? By searching for them in my file browser and hoping like heck I'll remember what I saved them as.

Would a more detailed and categorized file system actually work for me? Not likely. I've set up so many different systems in the past, and they all end up getting tossed into the "desktop rando stuff" folder eventually. I really want to get my computer perfectly organized, but, the truth is, I don't take the time to save and file things that way...it's just not me. I *wish* it was, I've *tried* to change, but in the end, it just never sticks. Instead, I need simple desktop folders for "photos," "marketing," "blog posts," "videos," etc., where I can drag and drop things and back them up to the server in case I accidentally delete something important. As much as I want to be a detailed person who loves organizational abundance, I need fast and simple solutions for everyday use. Should I feel bad about this and beat myself up over it? Of course not; life is too short to cry over file folders. It works for me, and that is all that matters.

It's time to let go of those preconceived notions of how things are "supposed" to look and how we are "supposed" to act. Just let 'em go.

Now it is time to take the Clutterbug test.

But first, some instructions:

Be honest! Set aside your fantasy self. We don't need that person to answer questions. You won't learn anything constructive or useful from him or her. You will only be picking the answers that describe what you *aspire* to be or what you *should* be, instead of looking at who and where you are right now. Maybe you love the idea of having perfectly organized closets with your clothing arranged by style, season, and color. Maybe you tell yourself that you will make this happen...someday...when you have more time, money, or space. If your clothing is currently in a heap on the floor, then the detailed and perfectly organized closet is your *fantasy* self, not your *real-life* self. Sometimes the expectations we put on ourselves are so ridiculous that they are completely unattainable. The only thing an unattainable goal will do is make us hate ourselves and be the excuse we rely on for never getting started.

It's time we design our homes and plan our lives based on who we really are and what really works for us, but that'll only happen if you are honest. I'm going to hold up a mirror and show you who you are, and I will show you how to use the inherent strengths of your bug to overcome your weaknesses. This isn't your traditional self-help book, designed to morph you into a better and shinier version of yourself. You are already *amazing* just the way you are, so answer the test honestly and take that step to becoming the badass home boss that you are destined to be.

One last note: When taking the test, realize that the state of your home is a combination of ALL the styles living there, including your spouse and children. When answering the following questions, think about the spaces that are predominantly maintained by *you*, as this will help you to get a better understanding of your own Clutterbug style. Let's get started!

What Is Your Unique Organizing Style?

You can also find this test on my website at www.clutterbug.com.

You enjoy reading:

1. Magazines or blogs with lots of pictures.
2. Nonfiction books.
3. Fiction books.
4. Newspapers or how-to books.

You find your biggest clutter issue is:

1. I have "stuff" everywhere.
2. Paper and important items.
3. Inside closets, cabinets, and spare rooms.
4. I hold onto too many things that may be useful in the future.

Your home usually looks:

1. A bit cluttered with things I use and love on display.
2. Tidy, with occasional piles of papers or things I haven't gotten to yet.
3. Very clean and tidy, but behind closed doors, closets and drawers can be a mess.
4. A bit cluttered with projects or items I am still using in some areas.

You find it hard to get rid of:

1. Things I find beautiful or love to look at.
2. Items that were expensive or still in good condition.
3. Sentimental items.
4. Supplies, tools, and other items that are still useful.

Your room usually looks:

1. Filled with my favorite things and items I use often.
2. Relatively tidy, but I sometimes have piles that I need to deal with.
3. Clutter-free for the most part, but closets, drawers, and hidden areas are a mess.
4. A bit cluttered with daily-use items that I leave out.

When it comes to cleaning your home, you generally:

1. Have to spend time tidying my home before I can clean it.
2. Keep my home clean and tidy.
3. Have a pretty clean house, and I enjoy tidying it.
4. Want to have a really clean home, but piles sometimes get in the way.

Your ideal craft room:

1. Bright and colorful, with all my supplies displayed in pretty containers on shelving.
2. Everything organized perfectly in separate containers inside cabinets.
3. Everything stored out of sight except for a few pretty accessories.
4. All my tools perfectly organized and easy to access on a pegboard.

When it comes to your home's appearance, you prefer:

1. Bright, fun, and full of visual abundance.
2. Minimal visual clutter and very functional.
3. Pretty, inviting, with minimal visual clutter.
4. Visual, functional, and organized.

Organizing systems that work best for you are:

1. Visual systems that are fast and easy to use, like hooks or open baskets on a shelf.
2. Detailed systems that are hidden, such as file cabinets or subdivided compartments.
3. Hidden systems that are easy to use, such as baskets in the closet or drawer dividers.
4. Visual systems that are carefully organized, such as pegboards or clear drawers.

Your biggest organizing challenge is:

1. I don't like to hide things out of sight; I'm afraid I will forget about them.
2. I just haven't scheduled time to organize some areas efficiently.
3. I tend to neglect hidden areas in my home, like storage rooms.
4. I hate putting things away that I am just going to take out again later.

If a friend called and said they were coming over in ten minutes, you would:

1. Make a mad dash, grabbing as much clutter as I can.
2. Neaten slightly.
3. Wipe counters, hide any mess, and scrub the bathrooms in a hurry.
4. Finish up whatever it was I was working on.

You prefer your daily-use items:

1. Out where I can easily use them and not misplace them.
2. Organized properly and put away.
3. Out of sight, but still fast and easy to find.
4. Visible and organized properly for quick access.

You remember things best from:

1. Visual pictures and instructions.
2. Reading and researching about it.
3. Someone showing me how to do it.
4. Figuring it out on my own.

Pick the sentence that best describes you:

1. I struggle to put things away when I am done using them.
2. I am a bit of a perfectionist, and I prefer minimal clutter.
3. I like my home to appear spotless, but I hide things away where no one can see.
4. I like functional spaces that make doing hobbies and working easier.

You like your favorite things to be:

1. Out where I can always see them so they don't get misplaced.
2. Stored or displayed properly so they will last.
3. Neat and tidy and displayed in an eye-pleasing way.
4. Organized in a visual and functional way.

You like to decorate your home:

1. With bold colors and artwork.
2. With minimal, neutral colors.
3. With current design trends.
4. With useful, functional pieces.

You would like your home to be:

1. Fun, bright, and cozy.
2. Functional and minimal.
3. Beautiful and minimal.
4. Practical and efficient.

What Clutterbug Are You?

Add up your answers. Are you mostly a 1, 2, 3, or 4? You may also be a combination of all of these organizing styles!

If you answered mostly **1**, you are a **BUTTERFLY**!

If you answered mostly **2**, you are a **CRICKET**!

If you answered mostly **3**, you are a **LADYBUG**!

If you answered mostly **4**, you are a **BEE**!

You may find that, though you are a combination of all four styles, one stands out to you in particular. You may also find that you tend to fall into *different* category based on different rooms in your home or workplace. This is typical, but I can assure you that there will be a clear front-runner for your organizing style as you continue reading this book. I recommend that you read each and every chapter, no matter what your test results are.

In the following chapters, I will unpack each of the organizational styles in detail and offer practical solutions to help you work with your strengths, create new daily systems, and yes, finally get your life organized for good.

I will also show you the magic of learning how to live, work, and organize with those people in your life who may not have the same organizing style as you. Follow me, and let's start your journey to an organized, clutter-free, and productive life!

Bee

Butterfly

Cricket

Ladybug

Chapter 3

The Butterfly

Butterfly

VISUAL
ABUNDANCE
·
ORGANIZATIONAL
SIMPLICITY

Bee

VISUAL
ABUNDANCE

ORGANIZATIONAL
ABUNDANCE

Ladybug

VISUAL
SIMPLICITY

ORGANIZATIONAL
SIMPLICITY

VISUAL
SIMPLICITY
·
ORGANIZATIONAL
ABUNDANCE

 Cricket

*Visual Abundance
and
Organizational Simplicity*

Photo Courtesy of Christina Dennis, www.TheDIYMommy.com

A Butterfly rarely focuses on the small details and instead tends to look at the big picture. Butterflies prefer to see their belongings for fear of "out of sight, out of mind."

A Butterfly Brain

A Butterfly is fun-loving, creative, and outgoing. Classic dreamers, Butterflies are "big-picture" thinkers and spend a lot of time coming up with great ideas and ensuring that they are doing things that they enjoy. Order, structure, and routine do not come naturally to a Butterfly's carefree nature, so traditional organization is usually an area that they struggle with.

In general, when we think of organization, one picture comes to mind: micro-sorted categories hidden away inside closed cabinets, closets, and drawers. Everything, from school desks to filing cabinets, is based on this one system—which is the complete *opposite* of how a Butterfly brain works.

In a world designed to accommodate one organizing personality type, it's easy for those who don't fit that mold to feel like something is wrong with them. **A Butterfly, more than any other "Clutterbug," has probably felt messy and disorganized his or her entire life.** When a child struggles to keep her room clean, instead of adapting her storage solutions to work with her brain type, we try to force the child to adapt to the current system. This rarely works, and frequently causes this child to be scolded for being messy or lazy. Don't get me wrong. Kids are messy, but this is different. As a parent, you need to look at yourself and the child critically and see how much is the messiness of youth, and what is due to her natural organizational type working against your expectations. Help her organize to her strengths and potential, to save your own sanity.

Unfortunately, being told (or telling yourself) that you are a naturally messy person can quickly become a self-fulfilling prophecy. Butterflies have the ultimate excuse for not putting their things away when they are done with them: **"I'm just a messy person."** I can't blame you for thinking this way; you have probably tried and failed to get organized so many times in the past that you have resolved to simply stop trying. The idea of organizing and tidying your home is so overwhelming and daunting because you *know* you won't succeed. This is your internal excuse, and you likely don't even realize that you're telling yourself this.

For those of you who see yourselves in this scenario, you are not a messy person, everyone just organizes differently! **Make today the day you stop assuming you are going to fail.** It's time to let go of the excuses and start understanding how your brain processes organizing. I'm going to walk you through how to work with your strengths to design a system that will *finally* get you organized for good.

But if you're sitting there thinking, "That doesn't sound like me, I'm not that messy, but the test said I was a Butterfly," let me clarify that not *every* Butterfly struggles with clutter. Many Butterflies have immaculately clean and clutter-free homes. Once you understand your style, you too can create visually abundant homes with simple organizing solutions that work for you.

Being a Butterfly in no way means that you are doomed to a messy home. Most of the beautiful photos in this chapter are from the talented and inspirational designer Christina, from The DIY Mommy (who is totally a Butterfly!). Christina is *by far* my favorite interior designer, and her YouTube channel, blog, and Instagram are filled with beautiful Butterfly spaces. Her home is bright and filled with visual abundance and simple organizing solutions. If you are looking for Butterfly inspiration, look no further than The DIY Mommy. You can visit her at www.thediymommy.com.

For the purposes of this book, I am going to focus on those Butterflies who have not yet embraced their organizing style and are currently struggling with organization.

Your Butterfly Metamorphosis: From Clutter to Clean

As a Butterfly, you are a very visual person who likes to see all your belongings for fear of them disappearing from your mind the moment they disappear from sight. There is a real anxiety that comes with putting your belongings "away," whether you realize it or not. Subconsciously, there is a part of you that believes that, if you hang your favorite shirt in the closet, you may forget you even own it. Most Butterflies have clothing on top of their dressers or on the floor, but their closets and drawers are practically empty (except for those items they rarely wear).

I suspect this fear and anxiety stems from years of *truly* having misplaced or forgotten about your things. My kids were all Butterflies when they were little, as are most small children. If I put a toy in a closet or on a high shelf, they would *completely* forget about it. It was like Christmas morning any time I pulled out something they hadn't seen in a few days. The toys they could see were the most special things in the world to them, but as soon as those same toys were out of sight, they were erased from their minds entirely.

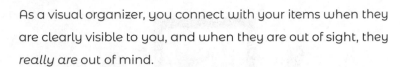

As a visual organizer, you connect with your items when they are clearly visible to you, and when they are out of sight, they *really are* out of mind.

I am about to blow your mind. Traditional organizing systems, being all about hiding away your belongings, are in nearly perfect opposition to how your mind naturally operates. *No wonder they have never worked for you.* Let the transformation begin! You now KNOW this magic thing about yourself and how your mind works. You have the answer to *why* you have always struggled to put your things away, and NOW you can design a visual system that works *with* your brain type to create a new habit of being tidy.

This in no way means that *everything* has to be visual. You are not a little kid anymore; you're not going to forget about *everything you own* if you can't see it. What really matters is the important, daily-use things. This includes keys, bills to be paid, your phone, calendars, reminders, vitamins, everyday medications, and anything else that you use frequently and that you deem important. This stuff needs to be kept visual. The anxiety about amnesia caused by absence translates to you leaving everything out in the open. *Don't worry*, the peanut butter can still go in the cupboard, but you *are* going to have to remind yourself to put it there after so many years of leaving it out.

Photo Courtesy of Sharon Carter, www.havenhomessc.com

The other side of the organizing conflict that Butterflies find themselves in is that most organizing solutions involve a micro-organized approach, which just doesn't work for you. The truth is, when you are done using something, your amazing brain is already onto the next thing, and it isn't going to stop to think about how to put that item away. If something is hard or complicated to put away, *you won't do it*. It's not that you *can't* do it. It just isn't going to be a priority, and therefore it isn't something that even enters your mind. You basically have organizational ADHD, but this isn't a bad thing. Your brain is usually going a hundred miles an hour, and as soon as you have the right systems in place, you can *finally* take off the emergency brake and leave your clutter problems in the dust.

Photo Courtesy of Christina Dennis, www.TheDIYMommy.com

A Butterfly needs easy, fast, and macro-organized solutions that are clearly visible to succeed. Let's take a look at a typical bathroom closet. The traditional image of organization would be stacked, separate containers for all the different categories and products. One container for pain relievers, one for allergy medication, and another for cold and flu...

Be honest with me for a second. If you have a headache and you dig out an aspirin, are you really going to take the time to take the lid off, put it back on, and restack the bins to put it away? Nope. You are going to leave it on the counter exactly where you used it.

Now, imagine for a minute that you could just toss the bottle back into one large, open container that holds all your different medications. Better yet, make this container clear so you can see exactly what's inside. Would you put it away now? It seems like an unorganized approach to organization, but trust me, this macro system is exactly what will work for you. Sure, you'll have to spend a few extra seconds digging through the bin for the aspirin the next time you need one, but you will also always know *exactly* where the aspirin is. Right now, you're probably asking yourself, "*Where was I the last time I took an aspirin?*" Taking a few extra seconds to find something isn't where you struggle, it's the putting it away part that needs to be easy. Taking a few extra minutes to create a LARGE label for this macro-organized medication bin is going to ensure that your brain registers exactly what is inside, which will alleviate the anxiety about forgetting or "losing" your things.

Bob the Butterfly

My first-ever male client was a full-blown Butterfly. For the purpose of this story, I'm going to call him Bob. The first time

I walked into Bob's home, it was instantly clear to me that his organizing style was Butterfly. Every surface was covered with random things. His table, kitchen counter, and even the floor had items, spread out and loosely piled, covering almost every square inch. There was a hall closet immediately to the left of the front door, but when I opened it, a single coat was on a hanger and the floor held only a few pairs of shoes. I noted that the stair banister (which was a full ten feet from the front door) had at least three coats hung on it, and Bob had a huge pile of shoes beside the front door. When I asked him about the coat and shoes in the closet, his cheeks flushed and he admitted to never wearing anything from that closet. He had no idea why he didn't use the closet; it just seemed easier for him to hang his coats on the banister or over the back of a chair instead.

Now, some of you may assume that Bob is just lazy. Why would he not just hang his coats in the closet? The truth is, he had to walk *farther* away from the door to hang his coat on the banister. It would have been *faster* and required *less effort* to just toss it in the closet. This wasn't about laziness; this was about Bob needing visual systems.

Bob's kitchen counter was covered in paper. Bills, newspapers, reminders...the pile had spread to over three feet wide. When I asked him why his paper pile had gotten so out of control, he admitted he hadn't noticed how large it had grown. Bob was so used to the pile, it had become invisible to him. He sheepishly explained that he wanted his papers to go in his office upstairs, but he never found the motivation to take them up there. The pile was too big, too overwhelming, and he simply couldn't be bothered to organize it. I see this exact same issue in almost every Butterfly home I visit. They either don't have a dedicated home for their daily-use items, or the items' "ideal home" isn't visual or easy enough to use.

Bob's office was too far from the front door to be a viable spot for him to drop his mail when he came home. In the absence of a dedicated "spot" for it, he piled it on the kitchen counter. Bob had tried, and failed, to organize his paperwork in the past. He had bought a filing cabinet and even purchased different-colored file folders. Setting up a paper system isn't where Bob failed; it was taking the time to use it every day that he struggled with. After years of failing, he had simply given up trying. Why should he continue to bother?

When organizing for a Butterfly, I design the space around eliminating all the excuses. Office too far away? Create a hanging filing system by the front door for mail and school papers. Is the closet not a visual enough option? Take the doors off and install hooks for coats and backpacks instead.

A Butterfly's home needs to be designed to transform the one-minute rule into the five-second rule. The one-minute rule is, If something takes less than ONE MINUTE to do, you must do it immediately. **For most Butterflies, if you can design a home where it takes less than FIVE SECONDS to put something away, they will have no excuses not to do it.**

For Bob's home, I designed his organizing systems based on his clutter hot spots. I hung a hanging file folder right beside his front door for incoming mail and clearly labeled it. I also hung a hook for his keys and installed a floating shelf to drop his wallet and phone onto when he walked in the door. I took off the front closet doors and installed hooks for his coats and baskets on the bottom, where he could just kick off his shoes. A simple basket labeled "Newspapers" beside his favorite reading chair eliminated the piles from his kitchen counter.

Photo Courtesy of Joan Mykyte

Bob's dirty clothes were piled in a corner of his bedroom, so that is exactly where I put a large laundry basket. I took down the empty medicine cabinet from above his toilet and installed open shelves for his bathroom products that were strewn about on the counter. I used clear containers...*lots* of clear containers, and I STILL marked them with huge labels to work with his visual organizing style. I macro-organized his home into simple, large categories and made sure that his daily-use items all had "homes" that were easy to put them away in and were placed EXACTLY where he used them most often.

We ditched the dresser in Bob's bedroom and opted for open shelving with large baskets instead. He was reluctant to take the doors off his bedroom closet, so we compromised and he agreed to leave them open all the time. I installed hooks behind his bedroom door for his "not dirty enough to wash yet" clothing, like jeans and sweaters...which were always hung on door knobs or laid on top of his dresser.

Photo Courtesy of Rachel Dowd, @SweetandSimpleHome

The end result was a visually organized home with an abundance of shelving, hooks, and clear containers. I also made sure to label EVERYTHING to eliminate Bob's subconscious excuse that he would "forget" about things if they were out of sight.

Let me tell you, nothing makes me cry like seeing a grown man cry, so Bob and I had our own little tear-fest when all was said and done. Bob had lived his entire forty-three years on this planet believing that he was lazy and messy, and would never have a clean house. His insecurity about his home had not only gotten in the way of his social life, it had interfered with his love life as well. He had never been married and had long since given up hope that he ever would. "Who would want to be with a slob?" This was the lie that he had told himself for so many years. It was his excuse for never putting himself out there and now that excuse was finally gone.

I'm not going to tell you that Bob transformed into a clean freak overnight. He had to work on changing his habits, and it took time and effort. The reason that Bob now has a clean, tidy, and organized home is that he now has a system that will not fail him. His home is designed to work *with* his organizing style, not against it. He has let go of the "slob story" he has told himself his entire life, and instead realizes that he is simply a visual organizer who needs macro solutions.

I wish I could tell you that Bob is now happily married, but the truth is, I have no idea. Bob's mother purchased my services for him as a birthday gift, and we have lost touch over the years. I still think of him from time to time, and when I do, I imagine him in a committed relationship with an adorable horde of little Butterflies of his own.

Maybe you can relate to Bob, or maybe your Butterfly brain struggles in other areas. The only thing that matters is that you understand what systems will work for you and why others have failed up to now. Knowing that you are a visual organizer who needs macro solutions is going to help you overcome your own "slob story" and see yourself for the organized and productive person you are. So let's dive into your strengths and set up a home designed just for you.

A Butterfly Breakdown

Still not sure if you are a Butterfly? Here are some common personality traits that Butterflies share:

- A Butterfly is a very visual person who likes to see all their belongings for fear of "out of sight, out of mind."

- Creative, carefree, and fun-loving are traits that are common to Butterflies.

- You are probably a Butterfly if you have clothing on top of your dresser and on the floor, but your closet and drawers are practically empty (except for items you don't use or love).

- A Butterfly focuses on the big picture, rather than the small details, in life.

- Butterflies prefer to have their items on display, even if subconsciously rather than formally, instead of being hidden in drawers or behind closed doors.

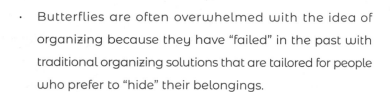
- Butterflies are often overwhelmed with the idea of organizing because they have "failed" in the past with traditional organizing solutions that are tailored for people who prefer to "hide" their belongings.

- A Butterfly needs easy, fast macro-organizing solutions, with items such as baskets or bins that are visible and/ or clearly labeled.

- Butterflies are emotionally connected to their belongings and have trouble letting go of them.

Butterfly Strengths

Butterflies are creative and intuitive thinkers who have fast-moving brains that often flutter from thought to thought. This is exactly why I chose the butterfly to represent this Clutterbug organizing type. Have you ever watched a butterfly go from flower to flower? They gracefully flutter in all directions, without any systematic approach to which flower they choose next. They are attracted to the brightest and most beautiful flowers, and they have an easy-going, relaxed nature. Butterflies don't need a structured and regimented routine to get their jobs done; they breeze through their days with a carefree joy.

You need to design your home to reflect the ease of a real butterfly, because that is exactly how your brain works. Your organizing style needs to allow you to float and flutter throughout your day and have your organizing systems reflect your carefree and visual nature.

Simplicity is your biggest strength. In a world filled with people struggling with inner perfectionism, you have the ability to look at the bigger picture. Your brain naturally groups things in larger, simpler categories, which naturally simplifies life. Your brain isn't focusing on and stressing about every small detail, and this gives you the ability to focus on other things, like creativity. A large majority of artists I have encountered have a Butterfly organizing style!

You can work with your natural style to create a simple, visual, and beautiful home that reflects who you really are as a person.

Here is what works for your beautiful Butterfly brain:

BINS, BINS, AND MORE BINS. You can find inexpensive, one-foot-square, clear plastic bins just about anywhere, but my favorite place is a dollar store. This is the perfect size of bin for those macro-sorted categories in your home. This size of container also fits nicely on most shelving units and in closets, so this will be a really versatile organizing solution for you. Of course, you may sometimes need bigger or smaller containers, depending on your space, but typically this is the perfect container for many different areas. I recommend getting a *lot* of them and using them *everywhere*. Use them to organize spices, medicines, bathroom products, snacks, toys, makeup, crafts supplies...and just about everything else. Be sure to keep the lids off—Butterflies have no patience for lids! By keeping your organizing solutions clear, you will be much more likely to use them, but if clear bins are not an option, labeling the outsides of your containers with LARGE and pretty labels are the next best thing for you. Your best solution? Clear containers that are also labeled!

LABELS. You need a visual reminder of what is inside your containers. Without this, you will forget what is inside and, even worse, you will be reluctant to put things away. You can use words or pictures to label your bins and baskets so you always have a visual reminder of what is inside. I also recommend labeling other areas in your home, not just containers. Labeling inside my fridge instantly led to things getting put back in the proper spot like magic! After years of hunting for the ketchup, one simple "condiments" label on the shelf in my fridge door meant we never had to look for the ketchup again. My family just started putting it back where it went. The label seemed to act like a subconscious reminder of where it properly belonged. This label magic works in every area of your home by motivating your brain to put things away, without you even realizing it! Use labels on every container and every shelf in your home to motivate you and your entire family to keep things organized.

KEEP IT VISUAL. You need to see your stuff: There is no way around that. I'm not talking about *everything* you own—that just isn't realistic—but your everyday things need to be visual. Use hooks, open shelving. and bulletin boards for those everyday items that tend to get piled on surfaces. Take a look at your clutter hot spots and ask yourself: "How can I design a visual organizing solution for this stuff?" Your creative brain will help you come up with the perfect visual systems, and you can also find a lot of inspiration on Pinterest and Instagram! Remember, though, you are the expert on your home and your family and, ultimately, your ideas are going to be much more effective for you than trying to copy someone else's system.

Photo Courtesy of Elise Fredriks

DECLUTTER. Butterflies tend to struggle with clutter more than any other organizing style. In my experience, clutter comes in two categories. One, things that don't get put away. This type of clutter is the stuff that collects on surfaces and in piles on the floor. Two, simply having too much stuff to begin with. Even when your belongings are put away in their proper home, if you have too much, it still counts as clutter.

The reason Butterflies struggle more than any other bug is twofold. First, they are reluctant to put things away for fear of forgetting about them, which leads to surface clutter *everywhere*. Secondly, these visually abundant bugs have more emotional attachment to their belongings, compared to those who prefer visual simplicity. When a Butterfly looks at their items, they see memories and value, even if the item is not sentimental or does not have much monetary value. This emotional attachment can make purging belongings very difficult, and it can cause extreme anxiety. If a Butterfly spends years acquiring new things, but never gets rid of the old, well, clutter overwhelms their home before they know it. Almost every hoarder I have ever worked with was a Butterfly.

Being a Butterfly does not mean that you will struggle with clutter forever! You can have an incredibly organized home; it is simply going to take *practice*. Decluttering will cause anxiety in the beginning, but, each time you force yourself to push through those uncomfortable feelings, it will be easier the next time. There are a few decluttering tricks that can help you let go a little bit easier:

- Have a friend or family member help you with organizing projects to keep you on track and help you let go of items that you are struggling to purge. Use the four-sort method when organizing any space.

- Have four labeled or color-coded baskets, bags, or boxes handy. One for **Trash**, one for **Donate,** one for **Does Not Belong**, and one for **Keep**. This will help you stay focused, and the visual labels will make purging your items easier.

- **Have a clear vision for your space**. Take a "before" picture of the mess right now and then find a picture, in a magazine or online, of what you want your space to look like after you have organized it. Hang both of these in your room somewhere that is easily seen, and watch your motivation to declutter grow.

- **A "Twenty-One-Item Toss" every month** is a great way for Butterflies to purge. Grab a bag and race around to find twenty-one items to get rid of as fast as you can. Twenty-one is the perfect number: It's just big enough a number to push you, but not so large that you can't accomplish it in just a few minutes. Find old clothing, expired medications, cooking utensils you never use... Trust me, finding twenty-one things is much easier than you think!

- **Schedule tidying time**. Set a phone reminder for the same time every day and spend ten minutes doing a quick tidy-up. Use this time to put things back where they belong or find homes for those "homeless clutter" items. Not only will this help you transform your space, it will also help you make decluttering and cleaning as you go a daily habit.

- **Remember, stuff is just stuff**. Your and your family's happiness is much more important. Don't let your anxiety about letting go get in the way of what really matters.

Grab a garbage bag and fill it with donations. Do this often enough and you are going to find more time, more space, and much more happiness in your home. You deserve a clutter-free home!

Photo Courtesy of Christina Dennis, www.TheDIYMommy.com

Making the Transition from Cluttered to Clean

The biggest impact you can have on your home and your life is simply creating some new habits. The fact that your brain works in the complete opposite way of traditional organization means that you have never really *learned* how to organize the right way for you. Your past struggles and failures have led you to believe that you are a messy person, and it is this belief that has established your bad clutter habits. **You are in the habit of being messy.** You probably don't always put things away when you are done with them; you usually just drop things as soon as you walk through the door, and you may have even given up on cleaning and tidying altogether. *I don't blame you.* Insanity is defined as doing the same thing over and over and expecting different results. You know that you are not going to hang your coat in the closet every night when you come home, so your brain has stopped you from even trying. It would be *insane* for you to keep trying to use traditional systems that work against your natural organizing type.

The difference between your past and today is that you now have the knowledge and understanding of what *your* organization looks like. You can now design a home created just for your Butterfly brain, with hooks, shelving, and visual macro systems that are *not going to fail you*. It's going to take work and practice to get into the habit of using these systems. You are going to have to remind yourself to put the peanut butter back in the cupboard when you are done making a sandwich. You will have to install hooks on your bedroom door so that you stop tossing your jeans on the chair or the floor. You will need to make daily tidying part of your regular bedtime routine until it becomes second nature, but I can promise you, it *will* become second nature. You *will* become a tidy and organized person, and it *will* become effortless.

The amazing thing that comes with knowing your organizational style is that this is going to affect so much more than just your home. This visual, macro system can be used in your workplace too, and it is critical to keep working on increasing your overall productivity. We are going to talk more about organization in the workplace and productivity in Chapter 8.

I hope more than anything that you can now give yourself some grace. I'll never forget the words of wisdom bestowed upon me by a good friend of mine. I had said to her, "I wish I could travel back in time and tell my ten-year-old self that she is perfect just the way she is." My friend said to me, **"So, tell her. She is still in there. You are still that little girl and she still needs to hear that."**

Tell that cute ten-year-old you, who is sad because they feel so messy, that they aren't messy; everyone just organizes differently. Tell them that they are a visual organizer, and they are *perfect* just the way they are. I want you to know that you are not alone. I have received THOUSANDS of emails from Butterflies just like you who have transformed their homes and their lives, just by knowing themselves better!

Getting Started

You have spent too long living the lie that you are a messy person. It's time to rewrite your "slob story" and create and design the life that you deserve. This is a new chapter in your life, and it starts with letting go of the excuses and telling yourself that you *can* do this. I need you to be confident in yourself, and confident in your ability to transform your life through organization.

Start in your home. Your *external* environment directly affects your *internal* environment. When your home or office is disorganized and chaotic, you are going to *feel* disorganized and chaotic. We need to get your home in control and organized before you can master organizing your productivity, your finances, and your life.

You may be feeling overwhelmed and discouraged by the amount of work ahead of you, but I can assure you, you will begin to see progress immediately, and you will achieve your goals before you know it. It starts with one step. One small step toward your goal and then another small step the next day. Consistency is the key here, not perfection, not the end result. Focus on the small wins and the small goals. It's those small accomplishments that are going to transform your life.

Start in your bedroom. This space is the first thing you see when you wake up and the last thing you see when you close your eyes. **Your bedroom is your sanctuary and your retreat from the world.** It's also the room in your home that sets the tone for your entire day, every single morning. I spent so many years focusing on the areas of my home that company would see when they came to visit. My master bedroom was always my dumping ground, the place where I "hid" my clutter from guests. I went to bed every night staring at piles of laundry that I hadn't put away and feeling anxious about the work I still had to do. I woke up to piles of clutter, reminding me that I was failing miserably to get my life together. The instant I opened my eyes, instead of feeling refreshed and optimistic about my day, my bedroom made me feel overwhelmed and exhausted. It was madness.

Now, my master bedroom is my first priority. The rest of the house can be a disaster, but I need to go to sleep in a tidy and organized space so I can wake up ready to seize the day. As soon as I started focusing on my bedroom, I started seeing an immediate change. I fell asleep faster and woke up feeling happier. I got out of bed feeling like I had my life in control, and that feeling stayed with me throughout my day. The mind is a powerful thing. When we think positively about ourselves and our life, positive things happen. I'm not trying to get all "woo-woo" on you, it's just a fact that even my skeptical self cannot dispute.

Today, right now, I want you to take ten minutes and tidy your bedroom. Clear off the dresser top, hang up some clothes, and find a few things that you can donate. Make a list of items you need to help you organize your bedroom a bit better, like hooks, some clear bins, or a few labels. This isn't about completely redecorating your entire room. This is about taking a few minutes to make it more functional for you. Grabbing some masking tape and a marker and labeling your dresser drawers is going to make you way more likely to actually use them! Open up those closet doors! Declutter and purge unused items. You deserve a relaxing oasis. Don't overthink this: Just jump right in and make it happen!

Treat yourself to a tidy bedroom this week. Make this the challenge for yourself! There is nothing better than waking up each morning to a clean and organized space! You are going to wake up feeling proud, motivated, and ready to tackle the day...and the rest of your home.

Photo Courtesy of Samantha Dougherty

Butterfly Testimonials

" You are so right, my entire life I always felt like I was a slob! I always preferred shelves over a dresser, or hooks out in the open instead of a coat closet. I've even talked about taking the door off our coat closet and making it more open so we don't forget to grab things we need before leaving the house. I thought I was crazy for wanting that. I attached photos of our couch that is covered in clothes, my empty sock drawer and our half empty closet! I even asked my husband to take the quiz (he is also a Butterfly) and watch your video. He kept shouting, 'Omg, that's so us!' Haha! Thank you for making us realize there's nothing wrong with us, that we just like to see our stuff! "

—Britney, Florida

" My husband and I took your test on Monday and I almost started crying when I read the Butterfly description. Our house has always been messy, no matter how often we clean it. We have already hung hooks by our front door and a corkboard in our kitchen. Those two things have already made a big difference. We are actually excited to organize! Thank you. "

—Jackie, Minnesota

" OK. I took the test. I'm a Butterfly. That explains why the closet door that fell off of the track eight years ago is still leaning against the wall. Now that I can see my clothes, 50 percent of them make it back into the closet. (Ha, who knew!?) Thank you so much. I purchased a double wide shelving system from Ikea and donated my dresser. My clothes now go on the shelf instead of the floor. IT'S WORKING. The things you say about a Butterfly are *so* true! I feel really proud of myself and, now, everywhere I look, I ask myself, 'How can I Butterfly this?' "

—@Ms Drake

" I have never been able to keep my home clean for more than a few days at a time. It made me feel so bad about myself. I took the test and found out I'm a Butterfly. I spent an entire weekend decluttering and putting things away and it has actually stayed that way. My family can't believe it! I know this sounds silly, but when I stopped thinking there was something wrong with me, it just became easier. Thank you. "

—Elise, London

Chapter 4

Living or Working with a Butterfly

Mission: Possible

Of all the thousands of emails and comments I receive each week, "I live with a Butterfly, how can we blend our styles?" is the most common question by far.

A Butterfly's organizing style is the exact *opposite* of what people generally think of when they think of "organization." As a result, most Butterflies have failed to master the skill and habit of being tidy. These are the people who leave their empty pop cans beside the sofa or drop their dirty clothing in the middle of the bedroom floor, instead of putting it in the hamper. Butterflies struggle to put their things "away" and usually identify themselves as unorganized and even...dare I say it...*a slob*. They probably gave up trying to be tidy a long time ago.

This negative self-talk and resignation to being "messy" may not even be something a Butterfly realizes that they are doing. It's likely that they are in denial, and it's entirely possible that they even blame others for their struggle with organization. Many Butterflies have actually become "blind" to the clutter and don't see their space the same way others do. Some Butterflies can even feel safe and content when surrounded by clutter, which is why so many people use hoarding as a coping mechanism for pain and loss. Again, this is often something that they are not even aware they are doing.

Photo Courtesy of Alysha Baker

As a person living or working with a Butterfly, the most important thing you can do is to simply understand where they are coming from. Imagine what it's like to be a visual organizer in a world that expects you to put your things away out of sight. Imagine the anxiety that comes with forgetting about *everything* when you can't see it. I want you to understand how frustrating and humiliating it must be for a person who needs organizational simplicity to be chastised for not being able to use a micro-organized system that is the complete opposite of how their brain works. Imagine that, every single time you have tried to get organized in the past, you have always failed at maintaining it.

Butterflies struggle with the perception of what a tidy and organized home is *supposed* to look like because that perception is the *complete* opposite of how their brain works. Understanding and recognizing this struggle is the first step to overcoming it. Butterflies *can* be neat and tidy and they *can* maintain a clean and organized home, but your perception of what neat and tidy looks like must adapt to include systems that are visual and have simple categories.

If you are a Bee or a Cricket living or working with a Butterfly, you probably live in a constant state of frustration because of their inability to follow your well-thought-out and effective organizational systems. To your detail-oriented brains, putting the paid credit card bill in the file folder labeled "Credit Card" seems like a no-brainer. To you, putting things into their "proper" categories is what organization is all about; it's these categories that ensure you can find what you are looking for and you know exactly what you have. To a Butterfly, however, *simplicity* is key. Their brain doesn't work in small details, so Butterflies focus on the big picture. Often, they are visionaries and dreamers, and it doesn't matter how hard they try, being a micro-organized person will *never* come naturally to them.

Photo Courtesy of Christina Dennis, www.TheDIYMommy.com

Macro Magic

For a Butterfly, the magic is in the macro. Butterflies need big, simple categories for their belongings to be able to put things away quickly. Instead of separate folders for each one of the bills, Butterflies need one basket or bin labeled "Bills," where everything gets tossed. Yes, it takes longer to find the item you need with a system like this, but you *save* time when it comes to putting that item away...and putting things away is where the Butterfly struggles. With so many thoughts flying around in their beautiful brains, they are not even going to think twice about how to put their belongings away "properly." They need systems that enable them to just toss things where they belong without a second thought.

Butterflies are all about visual *abundance*. If you are a Cricket or a Ladybug, you crave visual *simplicity*. Surrounded by a Butterfly's craving to see their belongings, you probably get stressed out. Ideally, you would love your home to have clutter-free surfaces with everything put away where it belongs. I get it, I really do. As a Ladybug, I need visual simplicity just like you, and I feel completely overwhelmed when my surfaces get cluttered and messy, so I know *exactly* how you feel. If you live or work with a Butterfly, having their "stuff" spread everywhere could leave you in a state of perpetual frustration. Worse, particularly when dealing with a significant other, having to constantly pick up after him or her can lead to resentment. If this is indeed your situation, you have probably tried to "organize" their stuff a million times, just to have them never able to keep it up. The only way to save your sanity (and maybe even your relationship) is first to acknowledge your own frustration and resentment...and now...*let it go.*

Your past assumptions were probably along the lines of "(he/she) just doesn't care" or "(she/he) just isn't trying hard enough." The truth is, while maybe they have not been trying very hard, it is also true—and so very important that you accept and understand—that this lack of effort is a result of years of failure and conditioning which has built up a sense of defeat in your significant other. It was never personal, and it's certainly not aimed at you with the intent to hurt or disrespect you.

I don't want to make excuses, but, the truth is, it isn't their fault. A Butterfly is *never* going to be a detailed or micro-organized person. No matter how hard they try, or more likely how hard you try to make them, being organized like you simply isn't in their nature. Once you accept that their need for visual solutions is real, and incorporate practical solutions that suit their nature, you can make real progress. Remember, Butterflies truly will completely forget about their belongings if they are "put away." This often subconscious fear of forgetting something important drives them to leave *everything* out in the open. The result is often an accumulation of their belongings, which leads to clutter and mess. My hope is that you can see that the intention and the process that leads to this result is about *them*, not about *you*. Find a way to work with it, not against it.

Changes can be made, but not with begging, nagging, or threats. A Butterfly can transform into a clean and organized person with a few new systems...and a little bit of practice.

Here is the golden rule when combining Clutterbug styles: In a relationship with divergent styles, you should always default to the needs of the visual bug and to the bug who needs simplicity. A Butterfly is both visual and someone who needs organizational simplicity. That means compromising your home and workplace toward a Butterfly organizing system.

Before you chuck this book across the room and declare that I'm a stark raving lunatic, let me assure you that I am not suggesting you completely abandon the idea of having a clean home and join in the "leaving your crap everywhere" party. Nor am I implying that a Butterfly's tendency to create a huge mess in five minutes flat is acceptable; I am simply saying that the systems in place to stop the mess and clutter need to work with their natural style for you both to succeed. Or you could always just keep trying to turn them into you. How's that been working out so far? In the end, it's much easier for you to relax some of your "perfection" and detail-oriented systems than it is for them to adhere to them. It's also much easier for your home to feature a visual calendar or a bulletin board for important reminders than it is to expect a Butterfly to just "remember" things that are written in a planner or saved on an electronic device.

This in no way means that *everything* in your home has to be visual, nor does it mean that you can no longer use a micro-organizing system. I'm talking about compromising in areas that Butterflies use every day and the areas where your Butterfly struggles the most. I also recommend that you be in charge of some of the spaces where your Butterfly may struggle, but you do not. Perhaps you can take over paying the bills and organizing the paperwork, because you would rather have it micro-organized and that is something at which you excel. Maybe you designate a "drop basket" for your Butterfly, where they can place their random things throughout the day and *you* can take a few minutes each night to put those things back away in their micro-organized place.

There are really only three options when living with a Butterfly (that is, if you don't count the fourth option of ending the relationship):

1. Live with the mess;

2. Be in charge of the mess; or

3. Create solutions that are Butterfly-friendly, thus eliminating the mess.

There are a few simple, easy things you can do to make being tidy easier for the Butterfly in your life. The most important thing you can do is to label...*everything*. Does your husband leave his vitamins spread out on the bathroom counter every day? Grab a shallow basket, label it "Vitamins," and put it back on the counter. As a Ladybug, the idea of having a vitamin basket on the counter makes me cry inside, just a little, but for a Butterfly, so does putting those vitamins away in the cabinet. **They just won't use them if they can't see them.** When they have a designated and visual home, your Butterfly will stop leaving them *spread out* and start containing their things in a neat and organized way. Labels give visual organizers a visual cue of what is inside a closed, hidden space. Those visual reminders go a long way toward alleviating the stress that comes with "forgetting" about items that have been put out of sight. Labeled baskets for simple categories can solve a lot of your Butterfly's clutter issues.

You can have a beautiful and clutter-free home *and* include some Butterfly-friendly organizing options. There must be compromises on both sides, but it starts with redesigning the systems that are not working to be more inclusive of the Butterfly's natural style. Hooks at the front door, a mail basket on the kitchen counter, investing in some open shelving. Now that you understand what they need to be successful, you can work together to design systems that can make both of you happy. I can't tell you EXACTLY how to set up these systems; it really depends on your home, your stuff, and how your family uses your space. I want you to trust that you and your Butterfly *can* come up with solutions that will work for both of you, all on your own. Brainstorm together, search Pinterest for inspiration, and remember: **it's about progress, not perfection.**

My Sister: A Slob Story

My sister is 100 percent a Butterfly. She is a brilliant, clinical mental health and addictions therapist, a mom of three, and she even runs her own successful business on the side. She is bright, funny, articulate...and I adore her. **My sister also struggles desperately with clutter and disorganization.** Though she has come a long way, every surface in her home is usually covered with kids' artwork, bills, clothing, toys, and other random objects that either have no home or need to be put away.

I try never to offer my sister unsolicited organizing advice; it just isn't my place to do so. When I visit her home, I am there to see *her*, not her mess...so I zip my lips about it.

A few months ago, I really wanted to show my followers how to organize a Butterfly space, so I asked her if I could film her home. She *reluctantly* agreed.

Photo Courtesy of Christina Dennis, www.TheDIYMommy.com

I get it. Having your little sister come and help you clean your messy home is bad enough, but sharing your mess with the world on YouTube takes a lot of guts. She bravely allowed me to organize her kids' toys and her kitchen, and she let me film the entire process and post it on the internet. She has some serious lady balls.

I was crazy excited that I got to organize both her children's toy area *and* her kitchen, using systems that complement her Butterfly style. The children's toys were sorted in large bins with picture labels, and those bins were placed on open shelving for easy access. In the kitchen, we hung bulletin boards for the kids' schoolwork and art, and we hung a see-through wire basket for incoming mail. We also used a simple "Stuff to Go Upstairs" basket to contain the clutter that usually was dropped and spread on the kitchen island, and installed hooks for her car keys and purse.

While sorting her clutter, a common issue kept arising. This is an issue I see in most Butterfly homes: **she just didn't have designated homes for anything.**

On her kitchen island, as I started sorting the pile of clutter, I pulled out a package of batteries and asked her, "Where do your batteries go? I'll put these away right now."

Her response? "I don't have a spot where we put them...just toss them in the cabinet over there" as she pointed to a cabinet in her kitchen that was already chock full of random things.

"Why in the kitchen cabinet?" I asked.

"Because I'll see them when I open it to get my vitamins." This was her method for everything in her home: Keeping everything spread out so she could see it, or putting it in the cabinets that she opened most often so she could see it.

It wasn't just the batteries that didn't have a "home." It was everything from her bills to her spare change. Even her most precious keepsakes, like her kids' report cards, were without a designated place to call their own. Nothing had an actual spot where it belonged, which resulted in nothing ever getting put away.

Here is the issue: **My sister *thinks* of herself as a slob. This is the *story* she tells herself.** As a small child, she was constantly berated for having a messy room. She struggled to organize her papers and clothing in high school and university and, by the time she was a young adult, she had given up on the idea of organization altogether. **"I spend all this time cleaning and organizing and it just gets messy again in a few days, so why even bother?"** Her internal "slob story" stops her from even *attempting* to get organized. Nothing she does will make a difference, so why should she even try?

When I was at her home, it took just seconds to grab a large basket, label it "Kids' Memories," and put it on her bookshelf. Instantly, the piles of report cards and special artwork had a place to go. Why hadn't she simply done this before?

In my sister's case, as for most Butterflies I've worked with, the issue comes from not having the confidence to set up a new system, simply because nothing has ever worked before. Creating a "home" for everything you own is exactly what organization is, but for some people, it really is a foreign concept. Any time they have tried to create designated spots in the past, they have probably forgotten about whatever they put away or they struggled to maintain a micro system and therefore are fearful to do this again.

For my sister, her kitchen and her toy area were transformed with some simple labeled baskets and a few bulletin boards... **and those spaces are *staying* clutter-free with minimal effort.** Could she have created these systems on her own? Of course.

But her fear of failure and the anxiety that comes with hidden and micro-organization had stopped her from ever really trying in the first place. Now that she has had success with a visual, macro system, her confidence is growing, and she is slowly replicating these systems throughout her home.

Another issue that my sister struggles with is *consistently* doing housework and sticking to a tidying habit. The other day, during a phone call, she admitted to me: "After dinner, Devin always wants to immediately clear the dishes and clean up. I always try to convince him that we can do it later and play with the kids or do something fun instead." This is another *story* that she tells herself. She convinces herself that the reason she doesn't do housework or organize is that there are more important things in life.

What I said to her elicited an unexpected response: "Perhaps the reason you resist and rebel against tidying up is that you think you are bad at it. Maybe you associate it with failing, so you avoid doing it. It takes only minutes to tidy up the dinner dishes, and you can still have lots of time to play with the kids or do something fun. Maybe the truth is that you know you are a great mom, so you would rather do things that you know you are good at and make you feel good about yourself. No one wants to feel like a failure, so maybe you are subconsciously avoiding things that make you feel that way." Silence. I waited for her to reply and when she did not, I offered her a different explanation: **"You are not bad at housework. You are not a messy person; that is the lie that you are telling yourself, Jen. Your fear of failing is the only reason you are not having success."** This time, her intensely emotional response was one of relief and understanding.

A Butterfly can say that the mess doesn't bother them, but this is another lie they tell themselves. Detachment is a way of protecting and shielding themselves from the hurt and shame that comes with their clutter. Overcoming this feeling of failure will come when they start having success instead. Success begins with using solutions that work with their style, and replacing that negative self-talk of "I hate doing the dishes" with positive self-talk like "I love and deserve to have a clean kitchen."

Photo Courtesy of Christina Dennis, www.TheDIYMommy.com

Remember, this organizing thing is utterly uncharted territory for a Butterfly, so have patience. It's going to take them time to develop new habits and build confidence in using the new organizing systems. Fortunately, when these new systems work with their natural style, the Butterfly can finally stop failing and start being the tidy, organized, and productive person they were always meant to be.

You are also going to need to help your Butterfly purge. Visual organizers are just more emotionally attached to their belongings than other bugs. This naturally makes letting go much more challenging. Talk about their struggle and try to find their biggest *why*. Are they reluctant to purge and donate items because of financial insecurity? A past loss or trauma? Getting to the root of anxiety around decluttering can go a long way to overcoming it. We are going to talk more about overcoming purging obstacles later in this book.

The biggest impact you can have is to simply be their cheerleader and their support system. You can help them transform their self-doubt into self-confidence, and together you can design a new system that will save your family time and effort, and ultimately bring you closer together.

Chapter 5

The Bee

Butterfly

VISUAL
ABUNDANCE
.
ORGANIZATIONAL
SIMPLICITY

Bee

VISUAL
ABUNDANCE
.
ORGANIZATIONAL
ABUNDANCE

Ladybug

VISUAL
SIMPLICITY
.
ORGANIZATIONAL
SIMPLICITY

VISUAL
SIMPLICITY
.
ORGANIZATIONAL
ABUNDANCE

Cricket

———

Visual Abundance
and
Organizational Abundance

———

Photo Courtesy of Deborah Hutchinson, www.invitationsbyhand.co.uk

A Busy Bee is a very detail-oriented person who prefers to see their belongings for fear of "out of sight, out of mind."

A Bee Brain

An organized home is all about "having a place for everything and everything in its place." A Bee has no problem maintaining an organized home and even thrives with order and structure, but that doesn't mean that some Bees don't struggle with clutter. Order, structure, and organization are all wonderful things, but it takes time, energy, and a plan to implement them. It is during that implementation phase that a Bee might stumble.

Everyone is different, so I want to clarify that not *every* Bee is going to struggle with clutter. For many Bees, their detail-oriented nature is a positive trait that doesn't have a negative effect on their life at all. For the purposes of this book, though, I am going to try to help those Bees who do struggle.

A Bee's biggest strength can also be their biggest weakness: *perfectionism*. Being a perfectionist can be an amazing quality, and it's definitely something you need when it comes to maintaining a detailed organizing system. I mean, who doesn't want a perfectly clean and organized home? The downside of perfectionism is that it can easily lead to procrastination. **The one thing I hear over and over again from my Bee clients is, while they have big dreams and aspirations, they struggle to start new organizing systems or projects until they can do them right.**

It can be easy for a Bee to put off things until they have the "perfect" supplies or the right amount of time to dedicate to the project. Bees often try to come up with the perfect plan for what they want their system or project to look like, and it's this planning that can quickly turn into *overplanning*. **Overplanning is just plain *overwhelming*.**

While I'm all for having a plan before starting something new, overplanning and focusing on the small details can definitely get in the way of ever actually getting started. If you have been thinking about or planning something—*without any action*—for longer than it would take to actually complete the task, you're probably overthinking it. **If you struggle with procrastination due to perfectionism, it's time to stop overthinking and just start organizing.**

Often, before a Bee even begins the process of organizing, their mind starts racing with details, such as the number of containers they will need or whether they need to buy a label maker. A Bee can easily fall down the rabbit hole of planning and potential problems before they even open a closet or drawer. Instead of micro-planning your organization, start by focusing on just getting started with the first step.

The first step of any organizing project is a quick declutter of anything that is obviously garbage, recycling, or something you know you can donate. *Start small.* Choose just one drawer, shelf, or pile on your kitchen counter, and deal with it. Don't think about the entire project and everything you have to do; just focus on one step at a time. Once you've done a quick declutter, it's time for Step Two, sorting your remaining belongings. Take a few minutes and sort these items into categories, making sure you identify a few distinctly separate piles. The third step is going through and decluttering those freshly sorted piles, just in case you missed some things during Step One which could still be purged. Ask yourself, "Do I really need (item)?" Step Four is finding a permanent home for the items you've chosen to keep in those sorted piles. I recommend choosing a visual place for your most important or daily-use items. We will discuss how to find the proper homes for your belongings later in this chapter.

> *By planning step-by-step, as you go, you will never run the risk of getting overwhelmed or discouraged by the process.*

Bees can sometimes also have a fear of failure. The drive to have things organized in a really detailed and subcategorized way can be overwhelming. It can prevent a Bee from knowing what to do first, and this stops them from actually getting started. The fear of doing it wrong or making a mistake is exactly what often stops some Bees from taking those first steps toward a clutter-free home. **"What if I donate something I will need in the future?" "What is the best way to sort and organize my craft supplies?" "Exactly how many containers will I need, and what are the best ones to buy?" "I've sorted all my things into thousands of little piles, but what do I do now?"**

Yes, you can be a perfectionist while also living in a messy and cluttered home. In fact, in many cases, it is the perfectionism that is actually the root cause of the clutter and mess.

The other natural trait of a Bee is that they are visual organizers. Out of sight truly equals out of mind. Just like a Butterfly, there have probably been times in your past where you have set up a "perfect organizing system" (such as a filing cabinet) and then failed to use it in the long term. The reason organizing systems have failed you in the past is that they hid things away out of sight. Just like a Butterfly, a Bee thrives on visual abundance. **You need to see your belongings to remember them and feel motivated to put them away.** It's most likely a subconscious habit and the reason why you struggle with clutter in highly used areas of your home.

This fear of forgetting about items stored in a hidden system can cause a Bee to pile things into neat and micro-organized piles...*all over the house*. A Bee can also get anxious if any other well-intentioned family member tries to move or "tidy up" their piles. This combination of visual organizer and detail-oriented brain type can add up to a lot of clutter, very quickly.

I'm certainly not saying that *all* Bees struggle with clutter. Everyone is different, and we all have different challenges in our lives. I'm simply trying to illustrate the underlying issues that I have witnessed with many people who have the same organizing personality. Some Bees are amazingly organized and have completely clutter-free homes, while others are drowning in clutter and struggling with hoarding tendencies.

Before you start thinking that I'm suggesting that having a Bee-type personality is a bad thing, let me assure you, I most certainly am not. **The natural logic and analytical thinking of a Bee means that organization is in your blood.** Sorting and categorizing is *literally* how your brain naturally works. This means that once you actually set up a system that works for your personality type, you are going to have no problem maintaining it. In fact, "America's Most Organized Person," Alejandra Costello, has Bee tendencies. If you have never heard of Alejandra, you are in for a treat! Alejandra is a life coach and professional organizer who teaches people how to get organized so they can thrive. She focuses on helping people move beyond the emotional barriers to getting organized, combined with setting up visual organizing systems that are easy to maintain. Alejandra has a wonderful YouTube channel and website where she educates and inspires others through organization. You can see all her beautiful Bee organization at www.Alejandra.tv.

Photo courtesy of Jennifer Stone, @SevenSproutsFarm

As long as your organizing systems are visual, you're the person who'll take those extra few minutes to take the lids off your containers and put things away. You're the person who doesn't mind coming home and instantly sorting your mail, or spending those few extra seconds to put everything away as soon as you are done using it. This is a huge strength of yours, and honestly, it's something I wish I had. I am going to help you overcome the procrastination and fear of failure that come from perfectionism and, once you have, your home will finally reflect the super-organized person that you truly are.

My Best Friend Jess's Slob Story

My best friend Jessica and I met at work in our early twenties, and we've been two peas in a pod ever since. We stood up in each other's weddings (which most best friends can say). We were also not only pregnant at the same time, but actually had our babies on the same day (which not many best friends can say). Before you ask, no, it wasn't planned, and yes, it's totally amazeballs that our daughters have the same birthday. She is *my person* and I can't imagine my life without her. We are so much alike in so many ways...except when it comes to organization. Jess is literally my polar opposite, and our extreme difference was a huge driving force in identifying the four different organizing types.

My BFF is a total Bee.

Jess has always struggled with clutter. She has too much stuff, she hates letting go, and she is a *huge* perfectionist. When I used to think of a "perfectionist," I imagined a super-high-achiever with perfect hair living in a perfectly spotless home. I definitely thought that a perfectionist must totally have their stuff together. I daydreamed about being one...the complete opposite of my chaotic and messy self.

The reality is that, while a perfectionist may *desire* to have everything perfect, life often gets in the way. Sometimes what a Bee wants just isn't realistic, and instead of settling, a Bee often chooses to wait. This is exactly the struggle that haunts my friend Jess.

When she first got married and had her daughter, her family of three lived in a five-hundred-fifty-square-foot home. Let that sink in. I bet most of the people reading this couldn't imagine living in less than a thousand square feet. With no basement, garage, or much in the way of closet space, it didn't take long to fill up her tiny home.

Being a total Bee, Jess is super visual and likes to *see* all her belongings. She also enjoys a ton of hobbies. She loves to cook and bake, and she insists on having every kitchen gadget known to man. She is a late-night infomercial's dream come true. She also loves to craft, so she has a lot of tools and supplies that go along with her numerous hobbies. Sewing, knitting, bow making, painting...let me tell you, if there is a craft out there, my friend Jess does it. I barely have the time to write out the list of hobbies she has, let alone try to do any of them.

As a visual person, she also has a deep emotional connection to her things, so she struggles to let go of anything. When you combine her massive amount of stuff and her husband, daughter, and two big dogs in a five-hundred-fifty-square-foot home...it's a recipe for clutter disaster. While she did take advantage of wall space with floor-to-ceiling shelving, there is only so much wall space in a house that size.

When our daughters were about two years old, I started going through my own journey from cluttered to clean. I began transforming my home with organization, and every day I would call Jess, totally giddy, and share all the organizing tips and tricks that had worked for me. Jess tried some of my "*best organizing ideas ever*," but none of them ever seemed to work for her. All the things that were working for me were hidden and macro-sorted (because I'm a Ladybug). Instead, she needs visual and micro sorted systems (because she's a Bee). So here I was, giving her all these tips and ideas that were totally the opposite of her style, and she was like "Cas, that isn't even organized...you're full-blown crazy." It wasn't until I defined the different organizing styles that I realized my Busy Bee BFF needs completely different systems and supplies than I do.

After years of living in a very cluttered and very small home, Jess and her family have recently moved into a beautiful, big house. Her new home features four bedrooms, with a whopping total of three thousand square feet for her family of three to enjoy. That's double the square footage of the previous house... *per person*.

Here is where life gets real, though: She truly believed that moving into a much bigger home would solve all of her clutter issues.

Jess assumed that, because she would have six times the space and actual storage to put things away, she could finally have the clean and organized home she dreamed of.

It took Jess and her family less than six months to completely fill up her new home with clutter.

While the small home and lack of storage was definitely *one* of the reasons she struggled, it wasn't the entire picture.

The "slob story" that she told herself was that "*one day*," when she had the space, she wouldn't be messy anymore. She told herself that "*one day*," when she had more closets, a full basement, and a craft room of her own, her clutter issues would be a thing of the past.

I've heard this same story more times than I can count. **People blame their clutter on lack of storage or not having the right or "perfect" organizing systems. People blame lack of time, lack of money, or lack of space for their clutter, and the truth is, none of that really matters.** I've heard these same slob stories from thousands of families, and they are the same slob stories I used to tell myself.

Just one year after Jessica and her family moved into her new, big, beautiful home, I came to help her organize her craft room.

Let me tell you, we could hardly even open the door because of the mountains of junk that covered almost every square inch of the floor.

This wasn't a case of over-shopping; this was a case of perfectionism gone rogue. Jess was taking hand-me-downs from friends and family members, finding things at thrift stores or anywhere she stumbled upon something useful, picking them up, and taking them home. She was collecting and keeping so many things, not only because they could be useful someday, but also because she saw them in terms of the monetary value it would take to replace them.

This is something that a lot of Bees (and other Clutterbugs) do. Their logical and analytical brains often see items for the value that they *could* come to have. They tell themselves, "Yes, it's an extra spatula, but if my old spatula broke, I'd have to replace it for $5. Therefore, I'm saving $5 by holding on to this extra one, or even making an extra $5 by accepting one from a friend for free."

This is exactly what Jessica's brain told her when she was bringing home all these random things; she told herself that she was *saving* money or even *gaining* money by accepting hand-me-downs and not purging unused items. **As a visual organizer, she is also more *emotionally* connected to her belongings, so when it comes to getting rid of things, not only is she fighting the logical side of her brain, she is also fighting the emotional side.**

In her craft room, the piles of clutter were more than waist-high, with only a single path from one side of the room to the other. It had taken her less than a year to fill the space so completely that it was absolutely unusable. When I stepped inside her craft room for the first time, I actually started to cry. I was devastated and heartbroken for her, but I also felt as though I had somehow failed her. This was the one space she had talked endlessly about having since the day I met her, and now, fifteen years later, she finally had it and was unable to use or enjoy it because of her clutter problem. As a professional organizer and her best friend, I should have stepped in and offered help long before it got this bad.

I knew, in order for her to have a really functional space, we had to get rid of 75 percent of what she had. I also knew that this wouldn't be easy or quick for her. Even if we covered the walls with floor-to-ceiling bookcases, there was just no way to organize that much stuff. The only way to give her a functional space was to declutter and donate *most* of her belongings.

Because getting rid of things is extremely hard for a Bee like Jess, we started with trash. We dug through those waist-high piles looking for obvious garbage. This is an easy way to start decluttering because it is usually a totally anxiety-free approach. The first thing I picked up was a water pitcher with a huge crack in the side. It was one of those water jugs with the spout at the bottom and she admitted that not only did it have a crack, but the spout leaked, so it couldn't hold any liquids. To me, it was obvious that this was garbage. A brand-new one was just $20 at the store, and this one was cracked AND broken.

"We can definitely get rid of this," I said as I placed it in the trash bag.

Jess froze and looked terrified. "Wait!" she gasped. "Don't throw it out; I could use that for candy or powdered laundry soap... or buttons!"

Here lies the issue. She sees *everything* for what it *could* be—someday. The thought of letting go of *anything* that could be even remotely useful feels wasteful to her. For Jess, throwing out that broken water jug felt like throwing away $20 *and* a really cool and useful container.

Right now, a Bee reading this can probably relate to Jess. You may be thinking, *What's wrong with keeping one broken water jug?* The problem is that *everything* you own has a perceived value and potential use. All those little things add up to a *lot* of things, and before you know it, you are miserable and drowning in clutter in your own home. So how do you overcome the struggle that all Bees face when it comes to letting go of items? Practice.

This is why I recommend starting with trash, then moving to unused stuff and so on, to make room for the things that really matter. What I did with Jess to really help alleviate her anxiety about letting go was to create a huge "maybe" pile in the living room.

I said to her, "Anything you are not 100 percent sure you want to stay in your craft room, let's move it to the living room. It doesn't mean we are getting rid of it, we are going to make those decisions later. Only the things you know for sure you want to keep in here are going to stay for now."

Indecision is a huge issue for Bees. They are afraid to make a mistake, so they don't make any decisions at all! By removing the fear of failure and the anxiety that comes from having to let go of useful items, it was easier for her to focus on what she wanted to keep, rather than think about what she had to get rid of. It's important for Bees to take charge of their clutter and not be afraid to make mistakes, and there are strategies to do this in ways that don't feel impossible or frightening.

When Jess isn't sure what to do with something, she defaults to keeping it. "What's the best way to recycle this?" or "What if my kid's school could use this?" or "Which donation center is the best place to take this to?" When in doubt, she makes zero decisions and just kicks that can down the road for another day. Her perfectionism was getting in the way of her progress. By creating a "maybe" pile, we bypassed all that inner turmoil and were able to just focus on organizing her space.

Another issue I often see with Bees (and Crickets for that matter) is the fear of disposing of items incorrectly. Again, this comes from perfectionism. **I have had more clients than I can count obsess over the best place to recycle old electronics or torn and soiled used clothing.** Everything from empty boxes to fabric scraps can be a huge stumbling block when they focus on the "right" and "perfect" way to dispose of something. Sometimes, the garbage really is the best option. It's sad and wasteful, but holding onto garbage because you are afraid to put it in a landfill isn't a long-term option. The only thing you can do is try your best to recycle, donate when you can, and acknowledge that sometimes there just isn't a viable place for everything to go. Forgive yourself and focus on the positive, which is a more serene and relaxing home for you and your family.

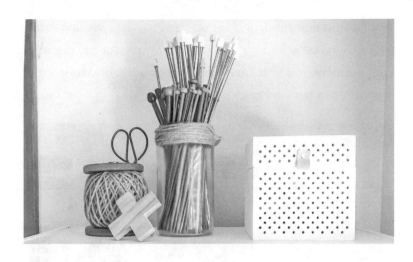

Photo Courtesy of Cassie Scott

As we sorted her craft supplies and put them into labeled containers, she let her inner organizing boss loose. I had to stop her when she eventually started organizing her push pins by their colored tops. Bees' tendency to *over-organize* can be really time-consuming. We started with big, macro categories...despite her desire to micro-sort. This was a much faster and easier way to tackle her piles, and we could go back and micro-organize the containers later (but I didn't let her sort her push pins by color). We installed shelving, hung a pegboard organizer, and set up her very own sewing table. After five hours of sorting and finding homes for her hoard of craft supplies, my best friend had a beautiful and functional craft room of her very own.

Photo Courtesy of Sarah J. Graber and Phyllis (Jersey) Medina

She was over-the-moon excited, and I knew that this was where the *real transformation* was going to take place; it was time to tackle the "maybe pile." As we stared at the HUGE pile of the things that she wasn't sure about, I simply said to her, **"If we put all this stuff back into your craft room, it's going to fill up the room again. It's going to make your beautiful, functional space cluttered and unusable."**

She hesitated. "But so much of this is really useful."

I simply responded, "Keeping all these useful things is making your space useless. You deserve to have your craft room. You

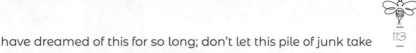

have dreamed of this for so long; don't let this pile of junk take that away from you. Nothing in this pile is worth more than you having the beautiful space that you deserve."

Having her craft room organized so perfectly made her decision to donate everything in her "maybe" pile much easier. It was now a *logical* decision to let it all go. She still fought me on the best places to dispose of everything. Even stray pipe cleaners, lone pompoms, and fabric scraps were spared the garbage bag because she insisted on taking them to her daughter's school, despite my insistence that they were all just garbage. The broken water jug? It was spared the trash for the school as well. Finally, I loaded up my van and took everything that was left to the donation center, so she couldn't change her mind! Let me assure you, though: We have talked about her struggle to let go of those things, and she has admitted to me that she *doesn't miss a single thing.*

Not only does she not regret purging and decluttering, but the process has shown her that her fear was irrational. She is decluttering the rest of her home and slowly overcoming the anxiety that comes with letting go *through practice.*

Jess is no longer looking at her belongings as what they could be *someday.* She made the mental transition from seeing items for what they *could* give her in the future, to seeing them for what they *are* giving her right now. **Holding onto unused items is taking from you, not giving.** They are taking your time to maintain them, your space to store them, and your happiness by cluttering up your home. When you can finally see the difference, it's easy to purge and only keep the items that make you feel happy and fulfilled today.

Photo Courtesy of Nicole Vogeli, fauvoegeli.blogspot.com

So, my Bee friends, do not keep a broken water jug that *could be* used for buttons...*someday*. Stop worrying about how other people could possibly use it, or even the best way to recycle it. I'm not against being environmentally conscientious, but a Bee's perfectionist brain can overcomplicate simple tasks like getting rid of broken things. **This overthinking leads to procrastination, indecision, and clutter.** *You deserve better.*

It's time to be selfish. It's time to think of your own happiness. Your clutter is making you unhappy, and it's time to let it all go.

Worst-Case Scenario

The best way I have found to overcome purging anxiety is to ask yourself, **"What is the worst thing that could happen if I get rid of this thing?"** Let's use the broken water jug as an example. What is the worst thing that could happen if Jess were to get rid of it? What if she finds herself in need of a way to store a ton of buttons in the future? Well, she could use an old pickle jar instead. Maybe she wants a cute way to store her liquid laundry soap when she redesigns her laundry room one day. No problem, thrift stores are filled with awesome large jars that would work, and they are just a few dollars. My point is, when you ask yourself the worst-case scenario, the answer is often: **"I can use something else I already have,"** or **"I can borrow it from a friend,"** or **"I can find it again second-hand."**

Simply asking yourself **what the worst-case scenario would be** is an easy way to cut through emotional anxiety and allow yourself to reason with the rational side of your brain.

I'm not going to pretend that purging is easy, but I can tell you that it gets easier. With each item you remove from your home, you are going to feel lighter and happier. Regular decluttering is also going to lessen the anxiety that comes from letting go of stuff with a perceived value or the fear that you're disposing of things wrong and being wasteful.

Photo Courtesy of Jennifer Stone, @SevenSproutsFarm

A Bee Breakdown

- Still not sure if you are a Bee? Here is a quick list of the most common personality traits:

- A Bee often has many projects underway and is usually a busy and active person.

- Bees are very organized and tend to be perfectionists.

- Most Bees are very hardworking and tend toward high achievement.

- A Bee is a visual person who prefers to "see" their important and frequently-used items, rather than store them away in closets or containers.

- A Bee has a detail-oriented and analytical personality.

- Bees like to keep their tools, papers, and other supplies out until they are finished with a job, often piling them until they have a chance to put them away "properly."

- A Bee's clutter issues tend to stem from piling items to be put away "later" and leaving unfinished projects out to be completed "later."

- A Bee generally has a hard time letting go of items that could be useful in the future.

Bee Strengths

You are a hardworking, intelligent, creative, and detail-oriented person. Industrious is a word I often use to describe a Bee, which is exactly why I choose a bee to represent this organizing personality type. A bee is a visual bug, attracted to the most beautiful and colorful flowers, but a bee also always has a plan. They work hard and are methodical in their collection of pollen and the construction of their hive. I also see the connection between the insect variety bee and the organizing personality type when it comes to crafts and cooking. A bee's hive is a brilliant home that they've meticulously crafted and, of course, bees make honey! I'm pretty sure that honey is bee vomit, but I'm making the correlation between it and baking, regardless. Almost all of my Bee clients have also been avid crafters who *loved* cooking and baking, so I saw yet another connection between the bug and the personality type I had assigned to it.

Perfectionism can also be a huge strength. Now that you are aware of the issues that come from obsessing over the tiny details, you can use your micro-organizing superpowers for good instead of evil (like when you actually have lots of time to make things super amazingly perfect). Self-awareness is such an important tool for change, and just by understanding your personality better, you can now work with your strengths to overcome your weaknesses. If perfectionism was holding you back, you can push yourself through the anxiety and fear of making the wrong decision and finally see real progress.

You also now know that you're a visual person, so you no longer have to waste your time setting up systems that are hidden. They just are not going to work for you. **Invest in pegboards and shelving with clear containers and, of course, lots of hooks.** You can still micro-organize your systems, but be careful not to over-organize your space when you first set up your new systems. I recommend always starting with a rough macro sort, because you can always go back and make those areas of your home perfect later, when you have more time.

My dad is 100 percent a Bee, and his garage is a total reflection of his visual and micro-organized personality. One huge wall in the garage is covered with a pegboard organizer, and he literally has outlines drawn onto the board for each of his tools. Clear jars filled with perfectly sorted nails, screws, nuts, bolts, and washers line endless shelves, and everything has a perfectly organized home. His garage is his happy place but, in the rest of the house, he lives with people who do not share his desire for perfection.

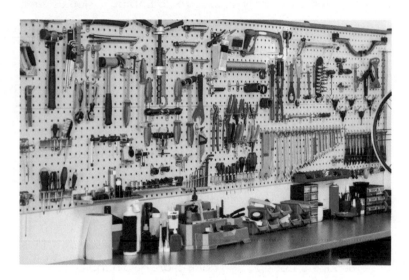

Fortunately, my dad has adapted his natural detail-oriented ways to be more accommodating to the rest of the family. This is exactly what I recommend you do as well. Take the time to set up your own personal spaces in a detailed and visual way, but make sure to compromise on the shared spaces in your home.

Remember, do not let your attachment to useful things make your space useless. Remind yourself that it's focusing on the here and now that is truly going to make you happy. Try not to look at each individual item, but instead at the space as a whole. If you haven't used something in the last twelve months, give yourself permission to stop feeling bad about disposing of it and move on. By having less, you are going to be able to have so much more free time to enjoy the many things that make your Busy Bee brain happy!

Decluttering is more than just having your home be more functional and inviting. Decluttering is about self-care. A messy house is stressful; there is no way to downplay it. You deserve a clean and organized space. As a Bee, you crave order and organization deep within your soul. Take the time to give yourself the space you crave. Purge, organize, and start truly enjoying your home.

I am in no way suggesting that you become a minimalist. Let's face it, Bees have a lot of stuff. **I call them Busy Bees for a reason!** Business owners, crafters, hobbyists...Bees are the work hard, play hard kind of people. Bees generally have a *lot* of hobbies. Reading is a hobby, so if a Bee is an avid reader, chances are they are drowning in books, magazines, or newspapers. Cooking and baking are also hobbies, so some Bees will have every tool they could ever possibly need in their kitchen. Bees almost always come with a lot of stuff. Whether it be exercise equipment, scrapbooking supplies, photographs, art supplies, books, cooking and baking utensils, woodworking materials, home improvement tools, or any other supplies you use for your hobby, it can quickly take over your space.

Don't worry, you don't need to get rid of it all. Simply look at the things you haven't used lately and make tough decisions about those things. Get rid of old, half-finished projects to make room for new and more exciting ones. Donate duplicate tools and supplies to make your hobbies easier to enjoy. Pass your

old hobbies onto a friend or family member to enjoy when you have moved on and no longer enjoy them.

Some other suggestions for a Busy Bee? Embrace good-enough organizing. It is better to start with a "good enough" organizing system (instead of piling); you can always come back and fine-tune your systems later, when you have more time. Second, try to have no more than three projects underway at once. If you have had an unfinished project for a long time, it may be time to get rid of it altogether and open yourself and your space up to new projects that you are more passionate about. Do you have a lot of exercise equipment that hasn't been used in years? As hard as it is, perhaps it is time to donate or sell that equipment and use the space for another hobby that you would actually enjoy, like a reading room or scrapbooking space. Do you really need that many pots and pans, screwdrivers, stickers, or books?

Photo Courtesy of Jeanine M. Haack

Bees are the masters of good intentions, but there are only so many hours in a day and only so much we can reasonably get done. There also comes a point when we need to admit that, even though something may be useful, it is taking up space that could be used for more important items. Here are some tips just for Bees:

- Make a priority list for yourself and your home. Is having a clean kitchen a priority over finishing your scrapbook? Then make time for what is a priority to you, and finish that task before you start a new one. Write yourself a to-do list and number it from most important to least. Do the MOST important ones first.

- Pegboard organizers would work amazingly well for your type. Put them everywhere.

- Clear bins, baskets, and jars should be your go-to organizing system.

- Invest in shelving. You are visual, so open shelving is a must for you. Bookcases are a Bee's best friend.

- Learn to let go. Bees tend to keep things "just in case" they may need it someday. If you don't love it and you haven't used it in a year, get rid of it.

- Schedule, schedule, schedule. Your time is precious, so make the most of it. Create daily and weekly chore lists, a daily schedule, and make sure you have a monthly calendar that you can reference easily.

- Bees can benefit from lists more than any other bug! Make a list of all the things you want to do that day (make it reasonable), and work on those and only those.

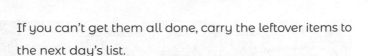

If you can't get them all done, carry the leftover items to the next day's list.

- Purge, purge, purge. Do you really need that many screwdrivers? Do you really use all those stamps? How many different kitchen gadgets do you really use on a regular basis? Bees collect things for their projects and often end up with rarely or completely unused items.

- Use project boxes. Have a box or basket with all the supplies you need for your current project. When you are done for the day, put the items back into the box until you can work on it again. This way, your supplies are out of the way, but you don't need to take everything out again to work on your project next time.

Now that we are at the end of the Bee chapter, I can already hear some of you yelling: **"But you didn't even tell me exactly how to organize my home! I want examples!"** Listen, Bee, this is exactly your issue! I may have a clean and organized home, but I can promise you that YOU are a much more organized person than I am. You already know the best way to organize your home; you just need to let go of the fear and get out of your own way. Trust your own instincts. Grab some clear bins or baskets, or label some that you already have, and just start sorting. Put the stuff you use the most often in the easiest place to access, and stop overthinking this!!

Photo Courtesy of Arcelia Fernandez

Go forth, my Busy Bee friend, and transform your home into an organized haven! Trust yourself and your beautiful, super-organized brain. You got this.

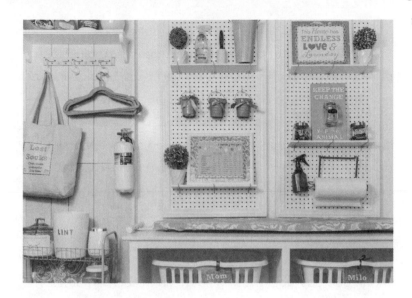

Bee Testimonials

" My husband is a Bee! This description fits him so well! He has three major, and a bajillion minor, hobbies. He literally has at least four times the amount of stuff that I (a Cricket) do. I'm reorganizing our house, starting with a living room. I've been trying to figure this part of him out for a couple years now, LOL, trying different systems. After learning his style, we went shopping for containers for the storage, he wanted the see-through bins, I wanted non-see-through bins that are labeled and color coded. Now I can figure out happy mediums: see-through totes with labeled, color-coordinated paper on the front face for open shelves, or closed-in shelving where you can just open the doors with all see-through containers. Thank you, Clutterbug! "

—Low Maintenance Momma, YouTube

"OMG, now that I know I'm a bee it makes sense to me that I procrastinate cleaning up... Uh...decluttering. I waited for the perfect system, but I never seemed to find it. I took your test, and then had a good long look at my office/craft room/library and...(drum roll)...it's based on the "Bee" principle. Craft books on this shelf, cookbooks on another, and so on. Even my tiny storage room shows it. Frequently used things are at the front and sorted into lots of categories. You encouraged me to go on with decluttering, because the way you explain it and talk about it makes me feel like a human "bee" and not like a mess. I will continue, but I am already seeing so much progress. Thank you Cas, you're doing so much in such an awesome manner. Your advice is the best I've ever received."

—Isabella, USA

"OMG! I think you are reading my mind! I am 100 percent a Bee. Yes, I AM a perfectionist. Yes, I totally struggle letting go of things because I may be able to use them someday! Yes, I want that perfect system, but until I have time, I'll just let the clutter accumulate. This is so me! Thank you for your quiz. I now completely understand myself AND why my daughters 'clean' the way they do. One is also a Bee and the other is a Ladybug. I see the light!"

—Nancy, Australia

Chapter 6

Living or Working with a Bee

The Hustle and Bustle of a Busy Bee

Bees are busy bugs and often have the "work hard, play hard" mentality. They are also fun and motivating people to be around. If you are lucky enough to live or work with a Bee, you know exactly what I'm talking about.

There's a kaleidoscope of extremes contained within the different facets of the Bee personality. Some are extremely visual, while and others need only their most important items out in the open. Some Bees are hard-core perfectionists, while others have learned to relax their standards and go with the flow a bit more. Wherever the Bee in your life is on the visual and perfectionist scale, I'm sure you can relate to his or her core underlying traits: hardworking, ambitious, creative, organized, and full-blown multi-taskers. A Bee usually has a lot going on in life, and almost always has a lot of *stuff* to go with it.

Photo Courtesy of Annie Wieler, @anniewieler

Living with a Bee

When it comes to organization, sometimes living or working with a Bee can be stressful, depending on the severity of the Bee's tendencies and how these differ from your own. **The biggest issue I hear time and time again from those who need help is that they tend to make a lot of piles, and really hate it when anyone attempts to move them.** This tendency to pile comes from a perfectionist nature. As a perfectionist, Bees want to put their items away "properly," so when time or space is an issue, they make a neat pile instead.

I get it, I do. As a Ladybug, visual clutter is the *worst*. When I see a pile, I just want to hide it. I can't tell you how many times I've "helped" my husband put his stuff away, only to ignite his frustration. My twelve years of marriage to a perfectionist has taught me this: **Don't hide the piles.** To my Ladybug brain, piles look like huge messes that need to be cleaned up fast. To a Bee, it's an organized collection of important things that need to be dealt with properly when there is time. Instead of hiding and shoving, it's best to encourage a Bee by helping her or him create clearly labeled "proper" homes for these piles. **Shoving and hiding is only going to lead to anxiety about losing things, which will intensify the piling in the future, rather than solve it.**

Photo courtesy of Gail Evans

Because of their perfectionist nature, a Bee can also have really high expectations of the other people who share their space. As micro-organizers, complex and detailed systems come naturally to them, and they often assume others will adapt. If you struggle to maintain a Bee's high level of organization, it can be frustrating for you both.

I once had a wonderful Bee client who was a single mom to three teenage children. This client (let's call her "Bethany") hired me to help "train" her children to pick up after themselves. One look at her meticulous home was all I needed to understand why she thought her children were so messy. Everything in Bethany's home was perfectly organized in stacked containers or arranged in perfect rows on shelving. If you needed a Band-Aid, you had to unstack four other bins which were on top of the "Band-Aid" bin, and then open various Ziploc bags inside, which were organized by size and type. Talk about intense!

To Bethany, her level of organization was normal and simple to maintain. To her three children (and myself), she may as well have been asking them to do calculus while blindfolded at a Backstreet Boys concert (just go with my analogy here, I was looking for something that would sound really tough). My point is, Bethany's children were not being messy because they were lazy; they just didn't organize in the same detailed and subcategorized way.

Now, it is true that not all Bees are as meticulous as Bethany, but they do all *strive* to be. This drive for perfection can often lead to procrastination. "Why bother if I can't do it right?" is something I often hear Bees say. So, while some Bees are extremely tidy and organized, others can struggle with clutter.

So, how do you work or live with a Bee-type personality? **With labels and lists.** Man, does the Bee ever benefit from having things written down! Not only do labels help overcome the anxiety that can manifest when visual organizers put their things "away," but they also provide subconscious motivation to tidy up. **As for making lists, nothing motivates a Bee more than having a proper and visual checklist.** A list keeps them focused and makes them much more productive.

A Bee requires structure and routine more than any other Clutterbug, whether they admit it or not. Their perfectionism can run rampant without a simple and attainable plan of action. Daily, weekly, and monthly to-dos can make living or working with a Bee so much less stressful. Because they usually have a lot going on, taking the time to write down their thoughts is important. Simply taking a few minutes to brain-dump their ideas on a piece of paper lessens the anxiety that comes with trying to micromanage their own thoughts all the time, and allows them to do one of the things they love best: organizing and applying structure, in this case, to their time and actions rather than their physical space.

The secret to making a list work for a Bee is to *prioritize* it. Bees want to do *everything*! While almost all Bees are already avid list makers, this doesn't mean that their current lists are effective. **A Bee MUST prioritize their lists.** Most Bees have high expectations of themselves and of others, but sometimes their expectations can get in the way of their progress. **Help the Bee in your life find success by encouraging them to brain-dump their ideas and then go through the list together, identifying the most important tasks.**

Priority Planner

Prioritizing Your Day Will Help You Achieve More

MY MOST IMPORTANT TASKS AND RESPONSIBILITIES

THE OTHER IMPORTANT/URGENT THINGS
THAT NEED MY ATTENTION

IF I HAVE TIME

THINGS TO DO FOR ME - PICK AT LEAST ONE PER DAY

Barb the Bee

A few years ago, I had a client (let's call her "Barb") who was 100 percent a Bee in every way. She hired me to help organize her kitchen and, let me tell you, our initial meeting did not go as she had planned. Barb's expectation was that we would discuss how to reorganize her kitchen in a more functional way. *Poor Barb*. She was in for a surprise!

Barb is a *superwoman*. Not only is she a stay-at-home mom to four children that she homeschools, but she also runs a home-based business *and* has her own blog. To say that she has a lot to manage is a huge understatement.

Despite having a massive kitchen, every square inch of her counter space was covered with piles of *stuff*. She had stacks of mail, kids' artwork, baking supplies, food storage containers, craft supplies, and more current *to-do lists* than I have ever seen.

The first thing I always do with a new client is simply sit and *talk* with them. I find out what they want from their space and help them identify what *is* and *isn't* working for them. I also want to learn all about their family. One of the most critical things I help them identify when we talk is the organizing personality of everyone in their home.

It took me less than two minutes to understand *exactly* why Barb's kitchen was a complete disaster, despite her being a very organized person. Barb wasn't prioritizing. Instead, she was trying to juggle so many balls that it was causing her to drop all of them! She was so utterly overwhelmed that she was spinning in circles. Worse, she had no idea how to stop the spiral.

Photo Courtesy of Indraja Panchumarthi

Here is how our conversation went:

Me: "Tell me how you want your kitchen to function. What do you want to use this space for?"

Barb: "Well, cooking and baking, of course. I have four kids and we eat all our meals at the kitchen table. I also run my business from here. I make cakes and cupcakes for clients, and usually every weekend I have orders to fill. Oh...and I homeschool at the kitchen table as well. I also started a blog, so I write at the table as well. And we pay our bills here...and this is where I like to craft...and I've been thinking of starting a catering business, so I do a lot of research for that in here too."

Her cheeks started to flush as she slowly kept adding more and more tasks that her family had assigned to the kitchen. It was as if she had never really stopped to think about everything she had been trying to accomplish, and when she finally took the time to list it all, it was instantly apparent that it was in *system overload*.

Both Barb's kitchen and brain were bursting at the seams.

She wanted to do it *all*.

Her expectations of herself and her poor kitchen were just not realistic. Instead of diving in and decluttering her counters, we sat and wrote a huge list of everything she wanted her kitchen to be used for.

Me: "Okay, Barb, I want you to write a number beside each item on the list. The number one is for the most important thing to be done in the kitchen, and ten is for the least important task."

Despite her perfectionist brain wanting to list *everything* as a one, she reluctantly sorted the tasks by level of importance. I helped her prioritize by asking "What *has* to be done daily?" and "Which items have deadlines and outside expectations?" and "Which tasks *cannot* be delegated to another space?" Here is a glimpse of her list:

1. Cooking

2. Eating meals

3. Baking cakes for business

4. Organizing cake orders

5. Homeschooling

6. Blogging

7. Surfing the internet

8. Crafting

9. Paying bills

10. Planning new catering business

Once we had her list prioritized, it was much easier to reason with her perfectionist brain.

Me: "We have to find another space, not the kitchen, for the bottom half of this list, Barb. Let's take a tour of your home and see what we can come up with."

Right next to the kitchen was a large and beautiful formal dining room. When I asked her how often it was being used, she reluctantly admitted that they only used it a few times a year for large dinner parties. Barb loved the *idea* of having a formal dining room and did not want to part with it, but now that she had her priority list, it was easy to see that creating a homeschooling space was much more important than having an unused room in her home.

Barb hired me to organize her kitchen and, instead, we transformed her dining room into a homeschool room that also doubled as her office for blogging and paying bills. We installed Ikea floor-to-ceiling open shelving for the children's school and craft supplies. We even moved the board games and some toys into this space. The end result was a gorgeous space that resembled a real classroom for her children to enjoy.

We also bought a beautiful large desk so Barb could work on her growing blog and business while her children worked on their school work.

With the school supplies and paperwork relocated from the kitchen into a new dedicated space of their own, Barb's kitchen now had more than enough space to cook, bake, and enjoy dinners as a family.

Here is the downside of being really ambitious like Barb: Sometimes, when we take on too many things in life, we end up not doing any of them very well. For Barb, being a great mother and running a successful cake business and blog were her top priorities, so that is where she decided to focus her time and energy. I encouraged Barb to put her dream of starting a catering business on the back burner, just for now. She wasn't giving up on it; she was simply setting it aside until the time was right to move it up her priority list.

Before I came, Barb had spent weeks thinking about the best way to organize her pots, pans, and dishes to have more space in her kitchen. She had wasted countless hours researching the best containers to organize her children's school supplies. She was so lost in the details that she couldn't see the bigger picture. She wasn't making any progress toward her objective.

Taking the time to step back and plan helped the bigger picture come into focus. Barb's priorities became clear, and the solution presented itself.

It's easy for a detail-oriented person to become lost in those little details. You may have a Bee in your life who could also benefit from taking a step back and reevaluating their home, their work space, or even their schedule. When someone is lost in a maze of indecision, the best thing you can do is offer a gentle hand and help show them the way out. You could offer to help make a prioritized list and encourage your Bee to write a plan for the *big picture*.

Photo Courtesy of Christa Schoolfield, @Schoolfieldchrista

Blending with a Bee

Remember the golden rule for blending organizing styles that was outlined in chapter 4.

When there is more than one personality type sharing a space, I recommend always defaulting to the *visual* and to the *simple* system.

As an example, this means it is much easier for an individual who craves visual simplicity (Crickets and Ladybugs) to go against their nature and learn to hang their coat on a hook than for someone who craves visual abundance (Bees and Butterflies) to put it away in a closet. It is also easier for a perfectionist (Crickets and Bees) who craves a detailed organizing system to relax their expectations and opt for a more macro approach than for someone who needs organizational simplicity (Butterflies and Ladybugs) to adapt to a complex approach. My clients who follow this rule have seen incredible success. It is hard, I get that, but you need to have an open mind and accept the need for compromise.

In the case of living with a Bee, the compromise requires the non-Bee to maintain a more visual approach for storage. However, if the other partner happens to be either Ladybug or Butterfly, then the Bee must in turn accept that the overall organizing system, though a visual one, is also simpler and less structured, to suit the other bug.

If you are reading this and find you need to defer to the visual Bee in your life (I'm talking to you, Crickets and Ladybugs), don't despair. I am in no way suggesting that *everything* in your home must be organized visually. I do recommend having a family calendar on the wall and a really visual place for incoming mail, keys, purses, and other daily-use items. You can still have a home that *feels* minimal to you, while maintaining a visual organizing system for your Bee. Opt for simple color schemes and invest in matching containers that are clearly labeled. Consider your Bee's "hot spots" for piling and try to create a visual system for things they tend to pile there. Hooks, pegboards, and open shelving are easy and effective visual organizing systems that work incredibly well for Bees.

If you are a Butterfly or a Ladybug, you may need to remind your Bee that you just are not a detail person and that you struggle to keep up with their level of organization. Having an open dialogue about your differences can go a long way to finding a great compromise.

If you are like me and get anxious when your home feels cluttered, explain to your Bee that their piles cause you stress, and ask them to consider "project boxes" or large baskets as a way of containing their piles until they have a chance to deal with them properly.

Remember, shoving their belongings in a closet or drawer (especially if you just went and did it without warning them— *sorry, honey*) causes them equal or greater stress and anxiety than you feel about their cluttered piles.

Compromise is key but, unfortunately, there is no perfect solution that will make everyone happy all the time. Combining different organizing styles is about give and take. It requires respect, patience, and lots of open communication.

The biggest hurdle that a Bee will have to overcome is the reluctance to let things go. Let me tell you, most Bees have a really hard time purging. To them, everything has a perceived value or a purpose. To a Bee, donating or throwing something away can seem wasteful.

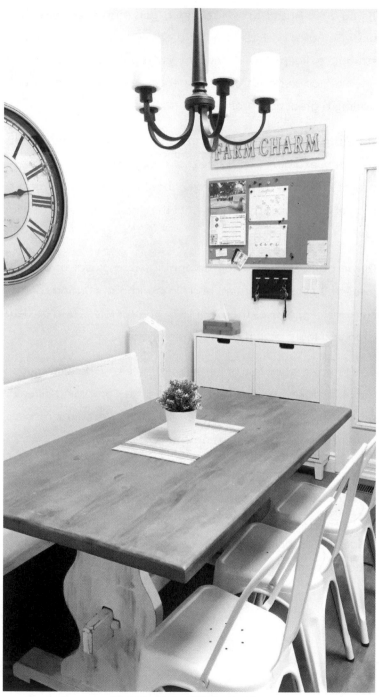

Photo Courtesy of Sasha Cushing

Lessening the anxiety that comes from purging is going to take practice. Be patient. I recommend starting slowly, with items that are obviously garbage. Be respectful and encouraging each time your Bee lets something go, no matter how small or meaningless it seemed to you. Congratulate your Bee when they get rid of old magazines, or offer to help sort and purge birthday cards that don't contain a special handwritten note inside. My sweet Bee grandmother used to keep every single greeting card she ever received, out of guilt; after some gentle persuading, she let go of hundreds of cards that only had loving words from Hallmark, not her family and friends.

Photo Courtesy of Mariana Kaczmarek, @marikaczmarek

Your support and encouragement will help your Bee overcome both their logical and emotional connection to their belongings.

Over time, the fear and anxiety of letting go will subside and your Bee will gain control over their collecting and piling tendencies.

Decluttering is harder for a Bee than it is for any other organizing personality type, but it isn't impossible. I've had Bee clients who are now full minimalists. Believe it or not, there are many professional organizers who themselves have a Bee organizing personality type!

When a Bee sets his or her mind to something and has a strong support system in place, anything and *everything* is possible.

Chapter 7

The Ladybug

Butterfly

VISUAL
ABUNDANCE
·
ORGANIZATIONAL
SIMPLICITY

Bee

VISUAL
ABUNDANCE
·
ORGANIZATIONAL
ABUNDANCE

Ladybug

VISUAL
SIMPLICITY
·
ORGANIZATIONAL
SIMPLICITY

VISUAL
SIMPLICITY
·
ORGANIZATIONAL
ABUNDANCE

 Cricket

Visual Simplicity
and
Organizational Simplicity

A Ladybug rarely focuses on the small details and instead tends to look at the big picture. This Bug enjoys a tidy space with minimal visual clutter.

A Ladybug Brain

Ladybugs are enigmas. Most of them tend to be carefree and outgoing, while at the same time being slightly neurotic and a total homebody. Can you be outgoing and never want to actually leave your house? Can you be fun-loving and carefree while also getting totally stressed out about dirty dishes on the counter? Yes, a Ladybug can.

Like the Butterfly, Ladybugs are big-picture thinkers. A Ladybug is a dreamer and rarely stops to focus on the small details in life. Fluttering from task to task, a fun-loving Ladybug can be easily distracted and requires simple and easy organizing solutions to stay on track. Their carefree and abundant natures are in stark contrast to the way they like their environment to look. Ladybugs crave visual simplicity, and they can get pretty intense about it.

As you've discovered in the preceding chapters, there are two kinds of people in this world: those who like to see their belongings and those who do not. A Ladybug is most undoubtedly a person who *does not* want to see their stuff, but taken to its most extreme.

I'm not talking about home decor items or furniture (being a Ladybug in no way makes you a minimalist). I am referring to all those things that we use, on any given day, that are not always aesthetically pleasing. I'm talking about your curling iron, the bills that need to be paid, or your bottles of vitamins. For a Ladybug, all those daily household items need to be tucked away far, far out of sight.

Now, let me tell you their most embarrassing secret. Ladybugs may *appear* to have a really organized home, but...*it's all a big fat lie*.

This may sound like a harsh statement, but I feel completely justified in making it because I am 100 percent a textbook Ladybug. I shove and hide everything out of sight, and my "cram it under the bed" mentality is a definite detriment to organization.

Just as having important items out of sight can cause some anxiety to visual organizers like Bees and Butterflies, having too many things on display can cause Ladybugs some serious heart palpitations. **Don't get me wrong, almost everyone will clean and hide their clutter before company comes over, but this does not make you a Ladybug.** A Ladybug does this even when *NO ONE* is coming over. To a Ladybug, they want their space constantly tidy for their own peace of mind. Unfortunately for this bug, the compulsion to have everything out of sight can drive them to hide even important items. Taken to its extreme, you can't function or find anything in your home. That makes their apparently tidy home an aesthetically pleasing illusion.

This tendency to hide clutter doesn't have to be a bad thing. With the right systems in place in our hidden areas, we can easily maintain an effortlessly organized home, even inside those dreaded drawers, closets, and storage areas. **That's the secret: having the *right* system for your organizing style.**

My Slob Story

I crave visual simplicity, with coordinating muted colors and lots of symmetry to keep my ADHD brain nice and calm. I may even have some (slight) obsessive tendencies when it comes to arranging the pillows on my sofa or the picture frames on my mantel. I've been known to straighten the bathroom towels multiple times a day, and I cannot have a burned-out lightbulb in my house without feeling a major eye twitch coming on.

Despite having the (obsessive) desire for my home to appear pretty and perfect, it only applies to the areas of my home that are plainly visible. **Behind closed doors, well, that's where I let my freak flag fly.**

I am a total slob. In my late teens and early twenties, my clutter was everywhere. My Ladybug brain was being entirely eclipsed by teenage angst, and I had honest-to-goodness *paths* carved through my piles of clutter to walk around. **By my mid-twenties, I had evolved into a total hidey-hoarder.** My "house cleaning" routine involved shoving and cramming my junk into every closet, drawer, and hidden space I could find. **Nothing was safe from my hidey-hoarder wrath.** Important papers? Good luck finding those among all the other random things crammed in my drawers. Clean clothes? Yeah...better do the sniff test, as they are all mixed with the dirty ones on the floor of my closet.

Obviously, there are different levels of crazy when it comes to Ladybugs. Some will have mountains of clutter fall on top of them every time they open a closet, while others are fairly organized, with just the occasional hidden area becoming an issue. Whatever your current Ladybug status, we all share the same common organizing traits: **We need visual simplicity along with organizational simplicity.**

Organizational Simplicity

For me and all my Ladybug *compadres*, we need really simple organization solutions in order to actually use them on a daily basis. I need the process of putting my incoming mail away to be as easy as shoving it in a drawer...*or else I'll totally just shove it in a drawer.* I've tried all sorts of wonderful organizing systems in the past: filing cabinets, binder systems, actual folders on my computer's desktop. I can use these sorted systems... *sometimes*, but, on a daily basis, I'm just way too distractible to take the time to get detailed. For us Ladybugs, it's all about the big picture, not the tiny details.

The real turning point in my clutter problem was the realization that simple, less detail-oriented solutions were the only way I could maintain an organized home over the long term. When I finally stopped trying to emulate the super-categorized, super-detailed systems I saw working for other people, I finally started to have real organizational success.

Photo Courtesy of Leslie Whitley

Hello, Hidey-Hoarder

Even before I became an organized person, I tried to take pride in my home's appearance. A pretty home is important to me, so decorating and DIY projects are my favorite hobbies. **I tried so hard to keep the top layer of my home under control, and this meant that the underside of everything was a huge, hot, freaking mess.** I really had no clue where anything was. EVER. I lost things daily and was constantly wasting hours pulling everything out of my closets, just to shove it all back in once the missing item was found. I remember all too well the panicked feeling of running late and not being able to find my keys or my wallet (or whatever other random but critical item I had lost). I would literally tear my home apart, looking everywhere, just to have to spend even more of my precious time hiding the piles away again when I was done. **I played this ridiculous hide-and-seek game _DAILY_.**

I honestly used to think that random strangers...or that sketchy neighbor or ex-boyfriend...must have broken into my home and robbed me when I couldn't find certain things. What kind of weirdo assumes that their left shoe MUST have been stolen because it is still MIA, despite having spent hours looking for it? _This weirdo, right here (pointing to myself)._ I would freak out _weekly_ over these random imaginary _"robberies."_ This was always an easier idea to accept than the truth, which was that I have never been robbed, my house was just a total pigsty. I couldn't find anything because I was completely and utterly disorganized.

Linda the Ladybug

My favorite client ever was a Ladybug, like me. Despite having permission to talk about her in this book, I'm going to refer to her as "Linda," for the sole reason that "Anne the Ladybug" just doesn't have the same ring to it.

Linda was a busy stay-at-home mom of two little boys and, like me, she had a real love for all things home-decor-related. When I first walked into her home for our initial consultation, my jaw dropped. *Linda's house was insanely beautiful.* I'm talking coffered ceilings, hand-scraped hardwoods, and enough magnolia wreaths to put Joanna Gaines to shame. Not only was Linda's home breathtaking, but it was immaculately clean as well.

Honestly, my heart sank. How could I possibly help this woman who was so obviously living at a Martha Stewart level of perfection?

We chatted politely as she led me through her magazine-worthy farmhouse-style kitchen and into her pristine great room. Because I have no filter whatsoever, I impulsively blurted, **"Linda, I can't help you. I am totally out of my league here. I organize my home with dishpans and dollar store bins; your home is already light-years ahead of mine."** Yeah, my insecurity about my own home and my low-budget approach to *everything* made me feel unworthy to help her.

Photo Courtesy of Sasha Cushing

Instead of looking shocked at my unprofessional outburst, she laughed and pointed to her hall closet. *"Go take a look in there,"* she giggled. The instant I slid open her magazine-worthy barn-style closet door, I sighed with relief. *Linda was a super slob like me.*

While the outside of Linda's home was at a level of clean and tidy that I could only dream of achieving, her closets were jammed with so much junk that I instantly knew we were sisters from another mister. It wasn't only Linda's closets that were disorganized. Even her kitchen cabinets and drawers were stuffed with papers, empty boxes, and just about everything else you could imagine. We actually found her son's filthy soccer jersey inside a salad bowl in her cabinet, at which she shouted: *"That's where I put that! It's been missing for two weeks."* There was literally no rhyme or reason to how anything was stored, and she admitted to spending hours looking for lost items all the time.

So how could someone who cared so deeply about her home's appearance shove dirty clothes inside a kitchen cabinet? That's easy: *Linda was a Ladybug.*

Here's the cycle that a Ladybug gets trapped in: **They spend so much of their time tidying up and looking for lost things that they feel like there isn't time to take everything out and organize it. Because they are not organized, they constantly have to tidy up and look for things, and so the vicious cycle continues.**

Linda was spending an average of three to four hours every day cleaning and tidying her home. She shoved and hid all the clutter because she just wanted it out of sight, but there wasn't an actual designated place for it to go. The result was a jumbled mess behind closed doors, where she wasted even more hours rummaging around for daily-use items.

Photo Courtesy of Samantha Dougherty

You've heard me say this before, so by now it shouldn't be a surprise: Linda's struggle (my struggle) is that *we Ladybugs don't organize in the traditional way.* Linda and I had tried hundreds of organizing containers and fancy systems in the past, but they had always failed us. We both assumed we were just naturally disorganized, and so gave up trying to organize long ago.

That is exactly why Linda had contacted me for help. She was tired of playing hide-and-seek, and she just wanted to finally get organized for good. When we sat for our consultation, I asked her the same question I ask all my clients: **"What is one organizing system that currently does work for you?"** Her response was truly heartbreaking.

"Nothing," she croaked, holding back tears. "You are the third professional organizer I've hired. The other wonderful ladies set up perfect systems in all my closets. You should have seen my pantry, it was so pretty. **I've spent thousands of dollars, but I just couldn't keep anything neat."** Linda wasn't making eye contact with me, and I knew what she was feeling all too well: *shame.*

To see this beautiful and talented woman in front of me feeling so bad about herself, *well,* it gouged me to my very soul. I knew *exactly* how she felt because I had been there. As a stay-at-home parent, caring for our home is a big part of the job. It seems like such a simple thing, keeping the house clean, so when you fail at it over and over again, you can't help but feel like a failure yourself.

Linda took pride in her home and worked hard to make it beautiful, but despite all the time, effort, and money she spent on it, she just couldn't keep it organized.

"Linda," I said, **"you are not messy. You are not disorganized. Those other organizing systems didn't work for you because they were not made for your organizing style; you're a Ladybug."**

Every time I meet someone who struggles with clutter and disorganization and I am able to explain to them about the different styles and why they have failed in the past, it's always such an incredible experience for me. I get to see that spark of hope in their eyes. I get to see that self-hatred melt away and be replaced by the self-awareness that they have been looking for. When someone *finally* understands themselves and realizes that there is nothing wrong with them at all, they stand up a little taller, smile a little broader, and their eyes shine a little brighter in an instant.

Despite our first meeting only being an initial consultation, I decided to spend just a few minutes transforming Linda's hall closet as a gift to her. We slid open the doors and pulled mountains of stuff out and piled it in the middle of the floor. Under the piles of winter coats, bulk packages of toilet paper, giant bags of chips, boxes of light bulbs and grocery bags stuffed with random clutter, I unearthed a closet organizing system complete with lots of shelving. On those shelves were dozens of small, pretty, labeled boxes, stacked in perfect rows. There were six boxes just for lightbulbs, with boxes for different types and styles. There was a box just for cleaning sponges and another for microfiber cloths. There were even individual boxes for each type of battery. Yes, the triple-A batteries had their own labeled pretty box. The other thing I noticed? There were lightbulbs and batteries sitting *in front* or *on top* of these boxes, instead of inside.

"That was the system the last organizer created." Linda commented sheepishly. Her cheeks flushed as she looked from the pretty, stacked boxes to the huge pile of stuff on the floor. **"It didn't even last a week before I started shoving things in this closet."**

Here is the problem I have with professional organizers: they organize the "*stuff*" in a home instead of organizing the *family*.

As a Ladybug, Linda would never take the time to unstack these boxes to sort and put things away in such a detailed system. Linda needs simple, fast, and easy solutions. Lids? She can't have any on her containers because she will rarely take the time to open them. Linda has to be able to toss and "hide" her things away in an instant, but in an organized manner so that she can easily find them again later.

I cannot tell you how many stories I've heard of families paying good money for professional organizing services, just to have them all fail a week later. If you (or the professional organizer) doesn't understand what systems will and will not work for you and your family's style, it can only end in failure.

The impromptu organizing of Linda's closet was all about showing her how a simple and easy system was all she needed. We ditched the pretty boxes and, instead, I had her round up some larger baskets and containers that she had stored in her basement. None of them matched, and I could see the terror in Linda's eyes when I started filling the mismatched containers with her things.

"It's just temporary," I assured her. **"You can go and purchase beautiful matching containers once we have a system in place that works for you. Function first, pretty later."**

Photo Courtesy of Christina Delp

Linda explained that she wanted this closet to be used as a place to store the food items she purchased in bulk, and as a spot for cleaning supplies, paper products, batteries, lightbulbs, and other household items.

Her face when I dumped all the sorted lightbulb boxes into one big container was priceless. She was even more horrified when I labeled that container with masking tape and a marker. I knew that, despite her closet now looking like a less-than-organized hot mess, it was exactly what was going to work for her.

In the end, we relocated the winter coats to the mudroom and found homes for all the other "homeless clutter" inside the closet. Each category was macro-sorted into a large container for things like lightbulbs, batteries, cleaning supplies, and paper products. The top and bottom shelves were perfect for those huge boxes of bulk food and toilet paper, and she even had an extra empty shelf.

It wasn't pretty, but it was organized. *Macro-organized*. At first, Linda wasn't convinced.

"But now, when I need a battery, I'll have to sort through that container for the size I need," she protested.

"Yes, it will take you a few extra seconds to find the battery you need, but you'll save that time when you put the package back away. It's the putting away part that you struggle with, not the finding." I tried to reassure her, but she still looked at me like I was totally insane.

I pulled down the battery container from the closet, took out a package of nine-volt batteries and put the container back on the shelf. When I handed the batteries to Linda, I simply had to say **"Now, put it away"** for her to instantly understand why this would work for her. Without moving from her spot and with minimal effort, she tossed the package back into the battery container.

To tell you the truth, when I left Linda's home that day, I had no idea if I would ever hear from her again. She now had a hall closet filled with mismatched and random storage containers that were labeled with masking tape and my messy handwriting. It was a far cry from the beautiful organizing systems that the other professional organizers had designed for her.

It was a full week before I heard from Linda again. When she finally emailed me, it was to request that I organize her *entire* home. When I showed up for our next meeting, she excitedly opened the closet we had impulsively organized on my last visit. The mismatched containers had all been replaced with gorgeous matching baskets, complete with pretty chalkboard labels. It was absolutely stunning, but it was still *organized* the exact same way. Linda had kept the large, macro categories because it was working for her and her family!

I spent two wonderful months helping Linda transform every hidden space in her home into an organized oasis. Her talents as a decorator made every closet Pinterest-worthy, but the macro-organizing systems also made them functional and practical for her and her family. I loved every single moment I spent helping Linda discover her inner organizing guru. **She had the exact same life-changing experience that I did when I first got organized: more free time, less stress, and way more self-confidence.**

No longer having to spend hours tidying (or looking for lost items) every day, Linda decided to take her extra free time and start her own part-time business as an interior decorator. We still keep in touch to this day, and her business is thriving, as is she. I am so blessed to have been part of her amazing transformation.

While not all my clients go on to start their dream career as Linda did, they all experience the life-changing impact that comes from understanding your style. I can't stress it enough that becoming organized is about making your life easier and less stressful. It's about freeing up valuable time and space, so that you can focus on the things that bring you happiness.

A Ladybug Breakdown

Are you still not sure if you are a Ladybug? Here are a few common traits that many Ladybugs share:

- A Ladybug loves to have a clean and tidy home, but their closets and drawers are usually a mess.

- Cluttered surfaces and messy piles can cause a Ladybug to feel stress and anxiety.

- "Cleaning the house" usually involves hiding and shoving things out of sight.

- A Ladybug doesn't have to have their things on display in order to remember them.

- Detailed systems like filing cabinets or stacked and sorted containers are an inconvenience to use.

- Family members often get upset when a Ladybug has moved or hidden their belongings.

- A Ladybug loves pretty, matching baskets and bins to contain and hide their household items.

- A Ladybug hides mail, medicine, and bathroom products out of sight, even when no one is coming over.

- Storage areas that are out of sight are difficult for Ladybugs to keep organized without the right systems in place.

Photo Courtesy of Lindsay Droke

Ladybug Strengths

Ladybugs usually have a great eye for design and love to make their homes beautiful. They also don't mind rolling up their sleeves and doing housework or tidying up messes, as it goes hand in hand with having a nice home. This is a huge strength! You are already in the habit of cleaning and tidying, which is typically a roadblock that many other Clutterbugs struggle with. Once your home is properly organized, you are going to be able to maintain it with little effort.

Simplicity is also a huge strength. In a world filled with people struggling with inner perfectionism, you look at the bigger picture. Your brain naturally groups things in large, simple categories, naturally simplifying life. Your brain isn't focusing and stressing about every small detail, and this gives you the ability to focus on other things, like getting stuff done! Ladybugs can accomplish a lot in a small amount of time.

I choose a ladybug to represent this organizing style for one obvious reason: A ladybug's shell is beautiful, shiny, and perfect, but underneath, it's a freaking horror show. Have you ever seen a ladybug when it opens its wings? It's all slimy and gross and they have these crumpled, jacked-up looking wings. Google it. Seriously, a ladybug represents this personality type perfectly!

Another cool thing about the actual bug is that they will follow any line that you draw on paper. It's really neat! Google "ladybug follows drawn line" and watch the clip. When I first saw a video of this, I felt even more justified in choosing a ladybug to represent this organizing style. Once a plan has been implemented, Ladybug organizers are really great at following and maintaining the system (as long as it's simple). This is another reason why daily planners, to-do lists, and schedules work really well for you!

Once I finally started macro-organizing my entire home, it started staying organized as if by magic. I intentionally started out *very* slowly. I probably only spent about fifteen to twenty minutes organizing my home each week, so it took a while to build up the confidence to take the training wheels off. In all honesty, it took me a FULL YEAR to get every closet, drawer, and storage space organized properly for my Ladybug brain. The time it takes you to organize your home will depend entirely on how much time you dedicate and how many things you have. Some Ladybugs can organize their entire home in just one weekend, while others prefer to take it slow and pick away at it like I did.

Now that my entire home is finally organized, maintaining it has been effortless. I spend a fraction of the time cleaning my home that I used to. I never lose anything. My stress and anxiety are considerably lower. But the best part is that I have way more time for the people and the activities I love. To say that organizing for my style transformed my life is a huge understatement. I am confident that it will have the exact same impact on your life.

Think of this as an investment. Every minute you spend organizing or decluttering a space is going to save you hours over your lifetime. You will be happier and less stressed, and the rest of your family will be positively impacted in the same way. So carve out some time to implement some much-needed Ladybug organization today!

Photo Courtesy of Famina Skaria, @thechackolife

Here are some organizing solutions that work well for Ladybugs:

- Schedule short bursts of time to organize, even as little as fifteen minutes, three times per week. Choose just one drawer or one closet to organize at a time. Ladybugs need quick and easy projects to keep the motivation and momentum going.

- Use drawer dividers or small open containers to group like things together inside drawers. Examples: Batteries, pens, tools, jewelry, makeup, tape, craft supplies, etc.

Using dividers or open containers means you can just open the drawer and easily toss the item in its home!

· **If it is hard to put away, you won't do it**. Make your storage solutions easily accessible and clearly labeled. Use containers *without* lids in drawers, closets, and just about everywhere else!

· Pretty baskets are your best friend! Ladybugs love an attractive, clutter-free home. Using baskets can keep your home looking beautiful and uncluttered while giving you an easily accessible spot to store smaller items. Use containers for toys, newspapers, cookbooks, office supplies, and so much more! Buying baskets and containers that match and are the same color can give a Ladybug that minimal look, while providing that much-needed fast organization.

· A binder or daily planner will work well for you. A pretty binder with clear plastic sleeves is a great way to hold important family papers like schedules, calendars, contact numbers, recipes, coupons, school information, and kids' artwork! A Bullet journal is a great planner option for you, as it allows you to create your own schedule and plan your way.

· Create zones in your home for your stuff. The key to success is giving all of your items a "home," then you will naturally put everything away properly. Make sure the "homes" are close to where you use them. Do you do homework and crafts at the kitchen table? Make sure your homework and craft supplies are located in the kitchen. Organizing your activity and storage into

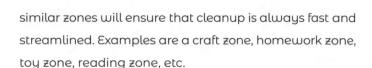

similar zones will ensure that cleanup is always fast and streamlined. Examples are a craft zone, homework zone, toy zone, reading zone, etc.

· Purge unused things often. Set a time once a month to go through and donate some items you are not using anymore. Your closets will be so much easier to keep clean with less stuff in there!

You're a Basket Case

Baskets and other containers are a Ladybug's secret weapon. Pretty, matching baskets (without lids) should be used *everywhere*! Every shelf, every closet, and every drawer should have containers so you can easily toss your things back into their homes.

A basket perfectly fits *both* of your organizational needs. First, it hides your belongings out of sight, giving you the visual simplicity that you crave. Secondly, it allows you to quickly put things away, without stuff becoming a jumbled, mixed-up mess. Containers will also hold a lot more items than just placing your items on a shelf, so you can double or even triple your storage space! Talk about efficient!

As an example, let's look at your bathroom closet. Without containers, bottles of medication, boxes of Band-Aids, and extra bathroom products can easily become a big pile all mixed together. When you use a container, you're taking advantage of the vertical space of the shelf, meaning you can fit a lot more in that space. If you have one container for "First Aid," one for "Medicine," and another for "Extra Products," you keep your macro categories separate, so it's super easy to find and put away your items.

Of course, labeling your containers is critical for long-term success. Labels also enable other Clutterbug personalities in your family to know where everything is. I can't stress enough the importance of always labeling your containers, no matter what your organizing style. This makes finding items and tidying up much easier, and they also act as a subconscious reminder to put things away when you are done using them.

Getting Started

As a Ladybug, you are already well on your way to having a clean and clutter-free home that is effortless to maintain. I recommend that you start your journey to organizing boss by decluttering and purging your hidden spaces. It's going to be so much easier for you to organize and maintain your closets and drawers when you have fewer things.

Fortunately, unlike other Clutterbugs, Ladybugs usually have less emotional attachment to things. Of course, we all have sentimental items that are hard to let go of, so always start with easy items, like expired medications, food, and bathroom products (like makeup). Here is a quick list of items that you can easily remove from your home right now:

- Clothing that no longer fits or you no longer love, and thus rarely or never wear.

- Books you've read and will not read again.

- Soaps, perfume, or lotions that you never use.

- Extra bedding or towels that haven't been used in twelve months.

- Old bills and statements.

- Kitchen items that haven't been used in twelve months.

- Expired medicine, food, and makeup.

- Toys your children have outgrown.

- Cleaning products that you don't like or rarely use.

It doesn't take long to do a quick purge of those hidden spaces in your home. Once you do, it will instantly give you the space you need to make your closets and storage areas just as beautiful as the rest of your home. What are you waiting for, my Ladybug friend? Put the book down and go purge something right now!

Ladybug Testimonials

" Before I knew what Clutterbug I was, I couldn't open a closet or drawer without stuff falling out. My papers were a mess and I could never find anything, but my house sure did look clean! Then I bought a Kallax Ikea 5 x 5 for my craft room, as well as ten baskets for the lower two rows. LOVE LOVE LOVE it!! Everything has its own basket, but no micro-organizing at all. Just one basket for photography stuff, one for paint stuff, one for sewing and so on. I've started putting rows of labeled baskets in all my closets and it's actually staying organized! Thank you Clutterbug! "

—Ellen, New York

" Just wanted to tell you how amazingly helpful the 'What Kind of Clutterbug Are You?' quiz has been for me. My husband and I have been married almost three years, and we are always feeling defeated about our messy house. It turns that I am a Ladybug and he is a Bee. We are complete opposites. I finally understand why we both get so frustrated with each other about the clutter and how to tidy it up. We are compromising with a more visual and less organized system and it's actually working! "

—Mary Anne, Texas

" I'm a Ladybug! It all makes sense now. I pride myself on having a clean house, but it's not organized at all. My basement is a junk pile and my closets are so full I can hardly use them. I'm starting small, like you. Last week I bought two baskets, one for my mail to read and one for bills to be paid. Such a simple concept, but I actually know where my bills are now! "

—Jenna, Facebook comment

Chapter 8

Living or Working with
a Ladybug

nest:

(n.) a place of retreat, rest, or lodging.

Feathering the Nest

A home is a sanctuary from the stresses and demands of the busy outside world. For most Ladybugs, there is a real joy that comes from decorating and cleaning their homes. Ladybugs take pride in and pleasure from feathering their nests, and those lucky enough to live with a Ladybug get to enjoy the benefits of typically clean and clutter-free homes.

A Ladybug works hard to maintain a tidy home, and as a result, tends to have high expectations of their family, roommates, and coworkers. Of course, there are different perceptions and standards for what it means to be tidy, but a typical Ladybug trends toward the extreme in a desire for clear surfaces and clean floors. I often hear Ladybugs say "I spend so much time cleaning, but the rest of my family never helps me," or "It's not fair that I have to do all the housework." I used to feel this way too.

A more realistic view is that, as a Ladybug, an extremely tidy home is just more important to me than it is to the rest of my family. It's not that they never clean, it's simply that their tolerance for mess is much higher than mine. I must admit, I do tend to clean *before* anything even appears to be dirty. How can I possibly expect others to adhere to my "invisible dirt" cleaning routine?

When I finally stopped looking at housework as something I did *for* my family or even *because* of them, I stopped being resentful. In truth, I clean and tidy for *myself*. I do it because it makes me happy to have a tidy home.

If you live with a Ladybug who is feeling resentful or upset that the rest of the family isn't helping out around the house enough, I recommend having a conversation about the level of cleanliness that is expected. Just as everyone organizes differently, everyone also has different priorities when it comes to cleaning their homes. Having an open and honest discussion about what you expect from each other is the best way to work out a compromise that everyone is happy with. Talk about what does work for each of you and what you would like to change. You can each make a list of the biggest concerns or challenges in your home and work together to brainstorm solutions.

In my home, I let go of the need for 24/7, high-level cleanliness because it simply isn't realistic. My family of five *lives* in our home, so there are often dirty dishes left on the counter, toys strewn about, and towels on the bathroom floor. I used to feel as though I was tidying all day long, and I probably was. Constant tidying is exhausting and a waste of my precious time. Now, all five of us spend a few minutes each night after dinner doing a quick house pick-up. Because of our family's **nighttime tidy routine**, we are blessed with a clean home each morning when we wake up. I no longer feel like the family maid, and my kids feel more comfortable and relaxed during the day without having to endure my "mommy meltdowns" over their mess. Deep breaths, Ladybugs, deep breaths.

Photo Courtesy of Lorena Corp

Playing Hide-and-Seek

Every time I watch reruns of old TV show *Friends*, I giggle at Monica's neurotic house-cleaning obsession. I can relate to her desire to have everything look perfect.

I also relate to her secret hidey-hoarder closet at the end of the hall.

Like most Ladybugs, I can get obsessive about my home looking tidy. The irony is that it doesn't bother me in the slightest to have closets, drawers, or storage rooms a complete wreck. Sure, part of it is the idea that company will come over and see that we actually sleep in our beds and eat on our dishes, but I also need that level of outer tidy just for my own piece of mind.

Visual clutter, or even a lot of different colors and patterns in one space, can cause me anxiety. I'm not alone in that reaction. Typical Ladybugs *crave* visual simplicity. **Muted color schemes and symmetry calm our chaotic souls**. I can't explain why having one lamp three inches too far to the left causes a Ladybug's blood pressure to rise, but a drawer in their kitchen that won't open because it's chock full of who-knows-what is no big deal. This weird combination of clean freak and super slob can leave other Clutterbugs scratching their heads. It would be like matter and antimatter coexisting in the same space. On its surface, it seems unnatural.

My husband calls me the "messiest clean person" he has ever met. I can easily get upset if he leaves the bills to be paid in a pile on the kitchen counter, but I have no problem filling the garage with garbage and recycling that I have not yet managed to take to the shed. Ladybugs are an enigma and, if you live or work with one, you know exactly what I'm talking about.

I asked my husband for help brainstorming some ideas for this chapter, since he has lived with a Ladybug for the past seventeen years. His response? "Get used to never knowing where any of

your s*** is, because a Ladybug is constantly going to hide it."
Sigh. Thus the truth is spoken. No one said it was pretty.

I still hide his stuff from time to time, but I really have gotten
better. At least I now remember *where* I've hidden it (usually).

One of the best Ladybug-friendly solutions we devised for
our home is assigning a "homeless clutter" bin to each family
member. When Joe or my kids leave one of their items out and
I'm tidying up, I simply put it into the appropriate person's bin
for them to sort through later.

If the Ladybug in your life has a tendency to hide your things,
I highly recommend placing a basket for each family member
in all the main living areas. My Joe has *multiple* "homeless
clutter" bins throughout the house because he has multiple
areas where he tends to pile. This reduces the opportunity
for the Ladybug (like me) to jam clutter just any old place
because the appropriate "homeless clutter" basket wasn't close
enough at hand. It also makes it easier for those affected by
someone else's cleaning impulses to find their stuff. In fact, if
the Ladybug can train their family to use the homeless clutter
baskets themselves, it will both reduce the amount of general
clutter and lessen the Ladybug's anxiety.

Photo Courtesy of Alexandra Simon, www.minimalistmaestra.com

A Long Line of Ladybugs

In chapter 2, I talked about my struggle with understanding the origin of the different organizing styles. *Is it nature or nurture?* I don't think there is a definite answer but, whatever the reason, I know that I come from a long line of Ladybug women.

My mom is the complete stereotype of a Ladybug personality. She prides herself on having a clean and clutter-free home, but hilarity ensues when she needs to find a pen. To watch her rummage through her many junk drawers, frantically scribbling to test each pen, just to toss the dry ones back inside the drawers, is truly a sight to behold. I also practice this pen-testing routine on a regular basis at my home, and yes, I also toss the pens that don't work back into the drawer so I can play the game again later. This Ladybug didn't fall far from the Ladybug tree.

Growing up, our home was always spotless, and my mom worked hard to keep every room really clean and clutter-free. But, as you've learned by now, **a clutter-free home doesn't necessarily equal an organized home**.

We lost things *constantly*. Important papers, keys, wallets, and clothing were misplaced as if on purpose. It's pretty much a yearly tradition that my mom will go to hide Christmas gifts and stumble upon gifts from previous years that she had forgotten about.

My grandmother is a Ladybug as well, and it's a long-running family joke that she would lose her head if it wasn't attached. Recently, she admitted to me that she used to hide kitchen clutter in her oven, only to forget the clutter was there until after she had turned on the oven some time later. My grandmother has melted a lot of stuff over the years, and the fact that she never burned her house down is a legitimate miracle. *Truth time: I have also melted many, many things by hiding them in the oven and forgetting about them.* Oh, Ladybugs.

The amazing thing about organization is that it can be learned at any age! Both my mom and my grandmother have learned to work with their Ladybug tendencies to create convenient homes for their belongings. They still "toss and hide" their things, but now it is done in a really sorted and organized way. Melting and losing items is a thing of the past for my entire extended Ladybug family, and it's all because we finally understand our natural style.

The Secret for Success

A Ladybug must work on letting go of their desire to hide away the clutter all the time. Just as it causes anxiety for visually abundant Bugs to have their things out of sight, a Ladybug can feel anxiety from having items left out in the open. A great way to combat this anxiety is to encourage them to leave other people's piles and clutter out for just twenty-four hours, instead of trying to tidy it up right away. Once they can manage to not touch it for twenty-four hours, ask them to try for forty-eight hours. Each time a Ladybug is forced to relax and suppress the need to hide, the anxiety about having items out will lessen. This approach is called "Cognitive-Behavioral Therapy" and has proven very effective for combating OCD and anxiety.

I am in no way suggesting that you try to persuade your Ladybug to be OK with a cluttered home. That's just never going to happen! This practice is about helping a Ladybug become a bit more respectful of other people's belongings and learning to give them a reasonable amount of time to tidy up themselves.

If you live with a Ladybug, their inability to use a detailed system can be frustrating. It didn't matter how many times my husband tried to get me to use the filing cabinet, I just continued to shove our paid bills into random drawers. It wasn't that I was maliciously ignoring his organizing system; I just couldn't bring myself to sort and file on a regular basis. My brain doesn't work like that. Instead, we opted for ONE open bin in the office labeled "Paid Bills." Now, my husband knows where everything is, nothing is misplaced, and we simply have to sort the papers during tax time. It's a win for me as well because I no longer have to fret over piles of paper, or feel the guilt and shame that come with failing to use his system.

For a Cricket or a Bee, they can open a drawer or put something on a shelf and keep it organized without any type of storage container required. Their brain naturally compartmentalizes things, so they can simply remember that shampoo goes on the top right shelf or that pens go on the left side of the second drawer. A Ladybug's brain does not work like that at all. Details and remembering specific places for things is hard enough, but also to stop and put effort into putting something trivial away "properly" in a closet just isn't going to happen.

This is where external separation and division comes into play. When you have multiple containers that are already sorted into large categories, a Ladybug doesn't have to stop and remember where something should go; it's already obvious. The containers also need to be open, without lids, and not stacked on top of each other, so that putting items away is fast and simple. This need for fast and simple solutions isn't linked to being lazy or unintelligent; rather, it comes from their tendency to focus on the big picture over small details.

> *While Crickets and Bees are task-focused, Ladybugs and Butterflies are time-focused. Crickets and Bees are all about doing something properly, while Ladybugs and Butterflies just want to do it fast.*

Because of this time-saver, get-it-done-and-move-on, "big picture" mentality, macro-sorted systems are the way to go. As I discussed earlier, you can help your Ladybug place open containers inside every drawer, closet, and storage area, so she or he can toss items into them without a second thought. Make sure these containers are labeled, of course, and there should be no problem maintaining the system long-term.

The other secret for helping your Ladybug get on the path to success is ensuring that the containers and other "homes" for things are located close to where these items are used. If you live with a scrapbooker who likes to work in the living room while watching television, scrapbooking supplies need to be kept in the living room, or at least close by. If you place the bin (or let your Ladybug place the bin) in a closet down the hall, that is too far away for the Ladybug brain to worry about taking the stuff when done. You will just find scissors and glue in the drawer under the TV stand and decorative paper shoved in the end table's drawer. Likewise, if the bills are dropped on the kitchen counter every day, the basket for the bills better be in the kitchen! It's a simple concept, one that many families are just not applying. Rearranging items to create simple, organized zones in your home will enable a Ladybug to stop hiding and shoving and start putting things away properly.

Lazy Larry: A Slob Story

Home is not the only place where people struggle with organization; keeping your work space running efficiently can be challenging as well. The first time I organized a professional workplace was for a client who happened to be a Cricket. This experience took me completely out of my comfort zone. My Cricket client (let's call her Carrie) ran a fast-paced textile business, so she needed an efficient organizing system that could keep up with her busy office. I was hired to create a detailed filing system for all the paperwork, office supplies, and hundreds of product samples. Micro-organization in a workplace setting is an intense and huge undertaking; it also goes completely against my natural macro-organizing style. This experience made me highly reluctant to do it again. However, when the opportunity to organize a work space came along, I agreed to at least meet with a potential client in the interest of gaining valuable experience and expanding my business reach. I walked in with my fingers and toes crossed that they weren't a Cricket as well.

Larry worked in an accounting firm with various coworkers and a huge client list. When I first walked into his personal office, it was neat and tidy, with a large wood desk, a wall of filing cabinets, and two comfortable leather chairs for clients to sit in. Diplomas and black-and-white photos of the city hung in perfect rows on his office walls. Larry's desk was completely clutter-free, except for his laptop and a photo of his beautiful family. I was stumped as to why he had called me.

We chatted about his three boys and their shared love of fishing. Larry had just bought his first boat and was gushing about future fishing trips he was planning with his family. He beamed as he told me about their various camping trips and how much he loved volunteering as his kids' Scout leader. It was clear that Larry led a full and happy home life. When I asked about his job, he smiled broadly. "I love my job," he exclaimed, and I could tell it was the truth. "It's long hours, but I hope to be partner soon." Larry's positivity was contagious.

It was only when I asked him why he had contacted me that his smile faded a bit.

"My boss encouraged me to hire a professional organizer," he admitted, obviously ashamed. "My assistant is frustrated with me, too. I've been known to misplace some client files from time to time."

"Show me what the issues are, and I can help you fix them." I was really curious about the sort of issues such a tidy and clutter-free space could possibly have. Larry opened his laptop and turned it around, so that I could see the screen. His desktop was completely covered in a jumbled mess of files. I'll be the first to admit that my desktop is a hodgepodge of icons, but Larry's existed on a whole other level of disaster that made mine look sparse in comparison.

"OK," I offered. "We need to come up with some electronic organization. No problem. Anything else?" Larry nodded sheepishly and led me to the rows of filing cabinets. As he pulled open the filing cabinet drawer, his office's hidden secret was revealed. Inside the drawer were dozens of files, stacked haphazardly. Pushed to the back of the drawer were hanging file folders, all with neat labels, all sitting empty. It was official; Larry was a Ladybug.

Here's the thing: I don't know the first thing about accounting or how an accounting firm would even need to file its paperwork. I don't know what's important to keep, and I certainly don't know what the day-to-day operations look like. **What I do know is how a *Ladybug organizes*, and I know that filing cabinets *do not* work.**

"Do you keep all your client files in your office?" I asked Larry, as he opened more drawers stuffed with papers.

"No," he replied. "I only keep the files that are open, the ones I'm working on right now. Once I've updated everything, the paper copies get filed back in our main filing cabinets. My assistant takes care of that."

Larry had dozens of files in each drawer. "You must have a lot of current clients," I observed.

Larry's cheeks reddened. "Not all of them are open right now," he admitted. "This first cabinet is for current files, this one is for the files that I need to finish entering electronically, and this cabinet is for the files that have been completed and need to go back in the main file cabinets." He looked embarrassed. "I need to sort them, I just haven't made the time." I could tell that his office was really bothering him. "I have a conference this week, so maybe we could get started when I get back. Let's check my schedule with Ashley, my assistant."

As Ashley pulled up Larry's upcoming schedule, it was apparent that he had little to no time to dedicate to reorganizing his office right now. He was booked solid with meetings after the conference, and the firm's busy time of year was right around the corner. As Larry and Ashley discussed moving meetings and shuffling his schedule around, I interrupted with a suggestion. "Can Ashley help me organize? Does she know which of your client files are current and which are not?"

Larry looked at Ashley, and she sighed with relief. "I'd love to help," she offered quickly. Obviously, her boss's disorganization was something that she was eager to overcome.

"Well, I guess that could work," Larry said nervously. "She is much more organized than I am, that's for sure. I know my laziness is driving her crazy and making her job even harder." **And there it was—that word that so many of us inappropriately use to describe ourselves: *lazy.***

Larry worked ten to twelve hours a day, and had even made time to volunteer with Scouts on evenings and weekends. The man was anything but lazy. How awful was it that his inability to use an organizing system (designed for Crickets) was making him feel that way about himself? **This is the part of my job that I live for: helping clients realize that the only issue they have is not using systems designed for their natural organizing style.**

While Larry was at his conference, Ashley and I spent a day reorganizing his office. We removed the filing cabinets and replaced them with beautiful armoire cabinets in the same wood tone as his desk, to maintain visual simplicity in the space. Inside the cabinets, we lined the shelves with shallow baskets, with labels like "Current Client Files," "To Be Entered," "Upcoming Meetings," and various other categories that Ashley recommended.

We put baskets in one cabinet labeled "To Be Filed," where Larry could place files as he finished with them, for Ashley to clear out at the end of each day. When a meeting was scheduled, Ashley could pull the main client file and put it in Larry's "Upcoming Meeting" basket for him, instead of on his desk. **When Larry's desk was kept clean and free from piled papers, he wouldn't feel the need to shove and hide all those papers when he "cleaned off" his desk each day.**

Ashley was a Cricket through and through. She could never understand her boss's challenge with operating the filing system she created for him. Once she understood how micro-systems just didn't work for his brain, she was able to completely embrace setting up macro systems for him instead. She even offered to help him organize his laptop into macro-folders once he came back from his business trip.

When Larry returned from his conference, he called to personally thank me for his functional, Ladybug-approved office space. I could hear his positivity oozing through the phone as he praised the system that was designed exactly for how his brain worked. I knew that this system would not only help him stay organized long-term, it would also help him overcome those feelings of guilt and shame that came from disorganization.

Living with a Ladybug

Let's talk about some more strategies for living or working with a Ladybug. Remember the golden rule for blending styles? **When there is more than one Clutterbug sharing the same space, always default to the *visual* and the *simple*.**

This means that a Ladybug has to be willing to let go of the need to hide everything and be much more open to visual organizing systems, like bulletin boards, open shelving, and hooks instead of hangers. **The rule also means that other Clutterbugs need to be willing to default to less detailed, more macro-organizing solutions in order for them to work for a Ladybug.**

As with every relationship, compromise is key. My husband would probably argue that he has compromised more of his Cricket style than I have of my Ladybug one, but the truth is that we have both come light-years in our quest to have our different organizing styles work together under one roof. We have "homeless clutter" bins in each room to collect his piles, so I no longer hide and shove it all in random drawers and closets. Every square inch of our home is macro-organized and labeled, so I never lose or forget where things belong. I've come to respect his personal space and no longer help him "tidy" his work bench or his paperwork that can sometimes be messy for longer than I would like.

Two of my children are Butterflies and one is a Bee. I've learned to respect their organizing differences as well, and we've designed and organized their bedrooms to reflect their unique styles. My eye twitches a bit to see every Lego creation my daughter has made proudly and loudly displayed on one shelving unit and all her Barbies displayed on another. As a Bee, she needs visual abundance to feel relaxed and happy, so that is exactly what her room offers her. My Butterfly babies need visual abundance too, along with fast and easy organizing systems, like lots of hooks and large labeled bins for their things to be tossed into.

Understanding my Ladybug brain has completely transformed my home and my life. When a Ladybug no longer tries to force herself into a Cricket box and instead embraces her true organizing style, she can finally have the functional, low-maintenance home she's been dreaming of.

So what are you waiting for? Run to the dollar store, grab some containers. and start macro-organizing your way to a clutter-free and happy home.

Chapter 9

The Cricket

Butterfly

VISUAL
ABUNDANCE
·
ORGANIZATIONAL
SIMPLICITY

Bee

VISUAL
ABUNDANCE
·
ORGANIZATIONAL
ABUNDANCE

Ladybug

VISUAL
SIMPLICITY
·
ORGANIZATIONAL
SIMPLICITY

VISUAL
SIMPLICITY
·
ORGANIZATIONAL
ABUNDANCE

Cricket

*Visual Simplicity
and
Organizational Abundance*

A Cricket is a very detail-oriented person who craves function and organization. This Bug enjoys a tidy space with minimal visual clutter.

A Cricket Brain

A Cricket is a classic organizer. **How their brain compartmentalizes things is the epitome of traditional organization and the exact style that most organizing systems and tools are designed for.** If you're a Cricket, lucky you!

Honestly, I'm pretty jealous of a Cricket's natural talent for organization. The reason I failed miserably at getting organized for so long was that I just couldn't maintain a detailed and abundant Cricket system. This is probably why the large majority of professional organizers are also Crickets. Organization just comes naturally to them. Their brains are already putting things into detailed categories, without their conscious participation.

A Cricket craves visual simplicity, which means they prefer a muted color scheme and minimal clutter in their home and work space. This is another key part of traditional organization. Most organizing systems are designed to sort and store items out of sight in bins, in binders, or behind closed doors. The recent minimalist movement is really appealing to a lot of Crickets too, as it closely aligns with their brain's natural organizing tendencies. Many minimalists are, in fact, Crickets.

Photo Courtesy of Nikki Boyd, www.athomewithNikki.com

The trait which most defines a Cricket is perfectionism.
They have a deep desire to do things the "right" way and
can sometimes be what people call a "type A" personality.
Logical, analytical, responsible, and organized—those are
the trademark traits of a Cricket. A detailed and functional
organizing system eases their anxiety about losing things and
ensures that they always know exactly where everything is
stored. **They share this perfectionism trait with the Bee, but
where Bees crave visual abundance, Crickets need visual
simplicity in their environment.**

Most homes are designed for a Cricket's organizing style. From the kitchen to the bedroom, *annoyingly,* storage is usually designed with them in mind. Dishes are meant to be hidden in cabinets, and clothing is sorted into drawers and closets. Almost every home offers storage behind closed doors, with the intent of placing micro-organized systems inside those hidden spaces. We sort our silverware, file our papers, and even schedule our time using systems that are designed to be hidden and detailed.

In a nutshell, how we function on a day-to-day basis in our world is, quite literally, designed just for you, my Cricket friend! Unfortunately, just because you can maintain organization easily, it doesn't necessarily mean that you always have an organized and clutter-free home.

Remember, everyone is different. Some Crickets have meticulous homes and never struggle with clutter, while other Crickets haven't learned how to focus their organizing superpowers and struggle to get started. If you are a Cricket looking for organizing inspiration, look no further than my friend Nikki Boyd from *At Home With Nikki.* Nikki is a professional organizer, YouTuber, blogger, and the most influential and inspiring Cricket I know! Many of the breathtaking photos featured in this chapter are from Nikki's beautiful and organized home. You can visit Nikki's website to see more of her Cricket organization in action on her website www.AtHomeWithNikki.com.

Photo Courtesy of Nikki Boyd, www.athomewithNikki.com

Perfectionism Paralysis

Sometimes, a Cricket's drive for perfection overpowers their need for visual simplicity. What this means is that, while they prefer to have everything out of sight, Crickets will often pile items until they have a chance to put things away "properly." There just isn't always the time or the perfect solution available for Crickets, so their piles can grow and spread easily while they wait for a better time to put things away. Just as for the Bee, **perfectionism leads to procrastination.**

So yes, Crickets are classic pilers. They make neat and organized piles with the intention of setting up perfect systems, or finding the time to put items away in the systems they already have. So, while their need for perfection overpowers their need to have everything hidden out of sight, their piles still cause them anxiety and unease.

Crickets also defy their natural organizing style when it comes to current projects they are working on. Many Crickets like having their to-do lists, or the tools and supplies for a current project, *visual* until the project is complete. Only then can they put their items away properly. Again, their need to do things the "right way" overpowers their need for visual simplicity in this case.

It's also easy for a Cricket to become overwhelmed with the little details in life. Overthinking and overplanning are common issues that a Cricket can struggle with. "Where do I start?" "How do I do this right?" or "What is the best method?" are all types of questions that Crickets ask themselves daily. Fear of failure is a huge stumbling block for Crickets and this fear can cause what I like to call ***perfection paralysis.*** Instead of making a mistake, the Cricket opts to not make any decision or take any action at all.

Preventing perfection paralysis with the Cricket is absolutely possible. This little story I am going to tell you next will show you how.

Cristina the Cricket: A Slob Story

I'm going to resist throwing my husband under the bus here (I'll save that for the next chapter) and instead talk about one of my very first clients; let's call her Cristina. Cristina was a retired schoolteacher who was now tutoring students from her home a few nights a week. She loved what she did, but her dream was to start a business working one-on-one with children and adults who are struggling with ADHD, Attention Deficit Hyperactivity Disorder. She contacted me to help her transform her spare bedroom into a fully functional office and classroom for her future students and business.

Cristina lived with her husband and their adorable cocker spaniel Tessa in a beautiful two-story home that was spacious as well as perfectly clean and organized—*on the main level*. Their second floor was a completely different story. As we walked up the stairs and rounded the landing, it was obvious what the organizational issue was. Despite Cristina and her husband not having any children of their own, there were children's books piled *everywhere*. The hallway was lined with neat stacks of books in every size, shape, and color. When she opened the door to her spare bedroom, a waist-high, colorful pile of what I can only describe as "stuff" greeted me. It looked like an entire school's worth of supplies was just dumped in the middle of the floor. There wasn't even a path to get to the other side of the room! I'm not going to lie, I felt a little weak in the knees.

Over a twenty-year teaching career, Cristina had collected a lot of classroom supplies. This was my first teacher client and, let me tell you, I swore it would be my last. Don't get me wrong, I love teachers and I think they are very undervalued and underappreciated professionals, but holy doodles, she had a lot of junk. When I questioned the sheer amount of stuff, Cristina explained that teachers had to supply *all* of the resources for their classrooms. She also explained that, when they switched to teaching different grades, they were responsible for buying all new educational materials for that classroom as well. After twenty years of teaching every grade from kindergarten to eighth grade, well, there was literally eight classrooms' worth of supplies piled in her room.

Let's talk about one of the *many* mistakes I made in my first year as a professional organizer: **I quoted the job instead of charging by the hour.** In Cristina's case, I estimated it would take us two full days to purge and reorganize her office, so I quoted her that amount. **Yep, I told her it would be $400 (plus supplies) to completely organize her new office/ classroom.** Of course, she quickly agreed! The contract was signed and I came back the following day to get started on her office transformation.

Two months later, I was still coming to Cristina's home a few days a week and, no, we were not even close to being done. Yes, I was still honoring my $400 quote, *and hell yes*, I was regretting it big-time.

What I hadn't accounted for was that Cristina was a Cricket. Only, she wasn't just any ol' run-of-the-mill Cricket. She was a perfectionist on steroids, with a strong opinion of "the right way" to organize. Every single item had to be sorted, categorized, and contained in the most detailed and micro-organized way. My brain hurt just being in the same room with her. Not only did she agonize over and second-guess every decision, but her expectations of herself, her space, and organization in general were just not realistic.

Cristina's desire for perfection was making her space messy and chaotic. It was the sole reason she had been struggling with an unusable office for over five years. It was the biggest roadblock in getting her business going. That is the dark side of perfectionism. It can flow so easy into debilitating indecision, procrastination, and chronic overthinking. So many people underestimate or flat-out don't understand how quickly it can take over and paralyze an otherwise bright and organized person.

Here's a typical conversation we had as we dug through her waist-high piles of stuff:

Me: I found a package of flash cards. Let's start a box just for flash cards.

Cristina: Those are sight words flash cards. They need to be kept with other sight word teachables, not just flash cards.

I labeled a box "Sight Words" and tossed in the package of flash cards. Then, as I came across a workbook all about sight words, I placed it into the sight words box too. This is where Cristina stopped me.

Cristina: That workbook can't go in with *those* flashcards; it is for a higher grade level.

When we first started to organize Cristina's space, I recommended that we sort by grade level. So, all the Kindergarten stuff together, all the grade one items together, and so on. She informed me that this wouldn't work, as a lot of items could be used for multiple grades and multiple learning levels. She also explained that her tutoring students had different learning levels in different subjects, so having things sorted by grade level wasn't an effective system.

I offered that we sort by subject, or teaching method, such as all the math items together or all the workbooks together. Cristina thought that these categories were "too broad." Her Cricket brain was craving a detailed and subcategorized system.

Me: OK, Cristina, where should we put the sight word workbooks for this grade level?

She had no idea, so we started a new pile.

After two weeks, everything was *everywhere*. Basically, we had just spread the mess from her office throughout her entire home into hundreds...and I mean *hundreds*...of tiny, micro-sorted piles.

There were over a dozen piles just for different items to help children count—math manipulatives, they're called—and, trust me, Cristina had enough for an entire school. She had dozens of piles for workbooks, but not just sorted by type; she had them sorted by subject and grade level, and then those were sorted by brand of workbooks. Cristina had sorted reading materials into piles by *letter,* and even had different piles for each vowel sound, depending on whether the vowel made the long or the short sound.

I was out of my league. I didn't know anything about teaching, so I allowed Cristina's determination to micro-organize everything to railroad me into a very bad situation.

Here is the problem with micro-organization: you *can't* do it first. It *has* to be the last step in the organizational process, or you'll end up like Cristina and me—two months and countless hours into a job with only a bigger mess to deal with.

We had piles. Lord help me, we had piles. There were *hundreds* of sticky notes labeling the piles throughout her entire home. *The entire process was completely nuts.*

We ran out of space upstairs, so the sorted piles spread down into the main floor living room, dining area, and even the kitchen. *My cheeks are hot as I type this.* I'm so embarrassed that I let this happen, and that embarrassment is still as fresh as it was all those years ago.

As we pulled items from her main pile, we would have to stop and agonize over what categories they should go into. Once we did decide on a category, we would then have to remember where that specific pile was located in her home. Remember, we had hundreds of piles to keep track of. *Nuts, I tell you.*

In the end, after two *very long* months (remember, I was only charging her for two days' worth of work), the entire room was empty and everything was sorted. So, now what? Where do we put all these hundreds and hundreds of tiny piles? Her office had a lot of great shelving, and even an empty closet that we could use, but it wasn't nearly enough space for all of Cristina's stuff. The sheer volume of categories was so immense that finding homes for all of them felt impossible. On top of that, how could she possibly keep track of where everything was, even if she did have the space? What if she needed a reading workbook for a third-grade student; how would she be able to quickly find that with over twenty-five piles of just different workbooks? I'm literally shaking my head as I write this because I can't believe I allowed the process to unfold into this nightmare of category overload.

You see, Cristina was a really organized person. In fact, she was *too organized*. Her drive to have everything meticulously sorted into micro-categories not only demanded a ridiculous amount of work that took up time and space, but it had left her with a system that could not function in any practical sense.

We had both fallen into the trap that so many Crickets succumb to: the Sorting Cycle. Crickets spend endless time sorting large piles into detailed categories, only to be left with lots of smaller piles. Finding functional homes for micro-sorted piles is tough, so they often end up getting mixed together again over time. Even if a Cricket does manage to find homes for all of those subdivided categories, it's often really difficult to keep track of where everything goes. Losing track leads right back into disorganization, and from there it is a short trip back to the beginning, the Sorting Cycle, to start all over again.

This was the "sink or swim" point of my own journey as a professional organizer. What Cristina thought she wanted wasn't realistic. I had to stand up and take charge of the situation, or end up sorting her home until the end of freaking time.

It was time to look at her space, not her stuff. I took Cristina into her empty office and asked her one simple question: "What *needs* to be in here? Not the stuff you would *like* to be in here, but what *HAS* to be in this space." She made a list of the basic office items she needed, and we brought each of those into her office and found homes on her shelving units.

Now we could see exactly how much space we had left to work with. It simply wasn't possible to have all her teaching supplies in this space, so I offered her another suggestion.

"What if we store your tutoring supplies on shelving in the basement? When you have a tutoring client, you can make them a custom basket, based on their learning level. That way you only need to store each client's basket in your office, and not all your supplies." Thankfully, Cristina loved this idea.

We bought industrial shelving and then macro-organized her piles and placed them into large plastic totes. Instead of one small container for each small category, we had a large tote for each large category. There were totes for math, sight words, craft supplies, workbooks, phonics, letter recognition, and various other macro categories. Inside each big container, smaller items were separated into categories and bagged for easy access.

In our journey of organizing Cristina's office, we had come full circle. We ended up settling on the exact macro method that

I had wanted to use on Day One of the project, and it took us only a few hours to actually get it done.

In truth, those two months of sorting and piling to the level of detail that we did was a huge waste of time, but I wouldn't go back and change it. Cristina learned the importance of macro-organization and, more importantly, the benefits of relaxing her expectations. I also learned *so* much from that experience. I learned how to help Crickets overcome their perfectionism and finally get organized for good.

A Cricket naturally wants to micro-organize first, but it always results in too many piles with no proper place to put them all. By starting with large categories, the initial sort is done much more quickly. Then, you can micro-organize to your heart's content within those broad categories. The lesson I learned from this experience has saved me countless hours and heartache with other clients, and hopefully it can save you time and effort as well.

The end result for Cristina's office was a functional and relaxing space, with room to grow her new tutoring and coaching business. Her closet had baskets tailored for each of her clients, along with empty baskets for the new clients to come. She had a library of books, work space for herself and her clients, and shelving with all the necessary supplies for day-to-day use. It was an airy, organized, and beautiful space.

Relocating her teaching supplies to the basement actually had more of an impact than the organization. It created so much open, usable space, allowing her to have the organized classroom and office she had always dreamed of. Her basement was also the perfect place to set up her custom learning lessons for each client. She could simply open each labeled tote and access the supplies she needed and put things back with ease.

Cristina was thrilled with the result, and I was blessed to have been able to learn so much from our experience. I saw the struggle that a perfectionist goes through, and this gave me the insight and tools to help other Crickets overcome their organizational challenges. Learning the importance of macro-organizing first was key to stopping the Sorting Cycle once and for all.

A Cricket Breakdown

Not sure if you're a Cricket? Here are a few common traits that many Crickets share:

- Until the "perfect" organizing system is put into place, a Cricket will often "pile" their belongings.

- Crickets tend to be described as having a "type A" personality.

- Crickets are very organized and detail-oriented people.

- A Cricket's mantra is: "Do it right, or don't do it at all."

- Procrastination is something most Crickets struggle with.

- Fear of failure, mistakes, and being seen as "incompetent" are roadblocks that prevent Crickets from achieving their dreams.

- Crickets tend to be very logical and high-achieving.

- A Cricket prefers minimal visual stimulation in their workplace and home, opting for a clutter-free and neutrally decorated space.

- Perfectionist is a title that most Crickets can relate to.

Cricket Strengths

I may have implied that a Cricket's perfectionism is a bad thing when, in fact, it's an amazing superpower to have. Just be sure you are using your superpower for good, and not evil. Your inner perfectionist is what motivates you and cheers you on from the sidelines. It's the fuel that powers your success and, quite frankly, I wish I had some of that perfectionist spirit. You are hardworking, organized, intelligent, and high-achieving. Your attention to detail is incredible and, when you put your mind to something, you can easily succeed at most things you try.

The issue arises when your inner dialogue shifts from "You got this, you can do anything" to "This isn't right, this isn't good enough." To counteract your negative self-talk, focus on the facts. Let your logical brain outsmart your perfectionism by asking yourself: "What is working? What is the purpose of what I am doing? Am I meeting that purpose? Is making a small mistake going to change the outcome?"

Once you learn to overcome indecision, and the negative self-talk that comes with it, your perfectionism makes you a force to be reckoned with.

I've had a lot of Crickets ask me why I chose this particular bug to represent their organizing style. True, a cricket isn't as beautiful as a ladybug, a butterfly, or even a bee, but a cricket is an insect dedicated to absolute perfection.

When I was in sixth grade, I did a school project on insects. Almost all the "good bugs" were taken by my classmates, so I settled on the cricket as the subject of my research. What I learned about these amazing insects stuck with me, and it's the reason I chose a cricket to represent this organizing personality type.

A cricket is nocturnal and, even at night, they prefer to remain hidden and out of sight. The most fascinating thing about this insect is, of course, *their song*. A male cricket makes its chirping sound by rubbing his wings together. Sounds rather plain and simple, but did you know that the rhythm of their songs is mathematically perfect? The steady and rhythmic song only changes during temperature fluctuations, slowing when it's cold outside and speeding up when it's hot. Do yourself a favor and Google "cricket song slowed down." Trust me, you won't be disappointed.

Photo Courtesy of Nikki Boyd, www.athomewithNikki.com

How to Use Your Powers for Good, Not Evil

When it comes to organization, once you have a stable system in place, you will have no problem maintaining it. A functional and efficiently-run home will save time and effort, and ease a lot of the anxiety that comes from having messy piles in your daily sight line. For a Cricket, it's all about creating functional systems and having a *simple and structured* daily plan of action. Not only will having an organized home dramatically improve your productivity, organizing your time will have an even bigger impact on your life.

As with Bees, planning is key to focusing and simplifying your overthinking brain. Taking a few minutes to write out your goals for the year, month, week, and day will go a long way to help you structure an action plan for your life. **Here is the key, though: Macro-organize your thoughts first, in the same way you need to macro-organize your home.** Create large categories for the items on your lists first, such as "Start a business" under your goal for the year, and then slowly break that goal down into more micro categories for the months, weeks, and your daily plan of action.

Photo Courtesy of Nikki Boyd, www.athomewithNikki.com

Overplanning and overthinking are issues for Crickets, so remember to keep your plan of action broad enough to allow room for changes and those inevitable bumps in the road. Even the best laid plans *never* go exactly as we think they are going to, so trying to plan for each and every detail is a waste of your beautiful brain's time and energy.

Though we all want our goals to become reality in an instant, the best things in life take time, mistakes, and persistence to achieve. When you see unfinished projects or errors that you've made, rather than judging how you are falling short, remind yourself that it's a work in progress, and a necessary step in achieving your ultimate goal. **Don't confuse the mess of the moment with failure. It's all part of the journey toward success.**

I also recommend being aware of your tendency to research *everything*. **Crickets love being well-informed before taking any action, but sometimes this focus on *learning* can take away from the actual *doing*.** Remind yourself that this tendency to overplan and over-research is your brain's way of delaying progress because of the fear of failure. If something is taking you more time to research and plan than it would to actually complete the project, *you're overthinking it*. **The best way to learn anything is by doing, and the greatest lessons you will ever learn will come from your own failures.**

Photo Courtesy of Wendy Lau, @thekwendyhome

Once you find the courage to jump right in and take action in your life, your perfectionism can be used to manifest incredible things and motivate you to accomplish your wildest dreams.

My best advice for a Cricket? Practice letting go a little bit. Embrace "good-enough organizing" by starting with a macro-sorting approach to your belongings. Here is an example:

Joe wants to put his financial paperwork into a filing system. He believes he needs a filing system for his investments, with separate folders for each year and investment. Joe also wants separate folders for each bank account and each of his children's education funds. In the meantime, all his papers are stacked in piles on his desk, and have been for *months*. A good solution would be to make one file called "Investments" and file everything together for the time being. He can always "micro-organize" this file folder at a later date and, for now, everything is organized, easy to find, and no longer taking away his valuable work space.

Here are some good organizing solutions for Crickets:

- Paper is your nemesis! Create a "good enough" paper filing system just to combat the piles.

- Invest in a paper shredder and use it...often!

- Use a basket or accordion file folder as a "short-term" filing system for your monthly bills and statements. Sort through these papers each year during tax time, shredding what you no longer need.

- Use a banker's box or filing cabinet as a "long-term" system for contracts and papers you need to keep longer than one year (like taxes).

- Label each file folder. Use general categories (Financial, Utilities, Insurance, Auto, School, etc.) in the beginning, until you have more time to make a detailed filing system.

- Be mindful of other "Clutterbugs" in your home or workplace, and be sure that your systems are simple enough for their use.

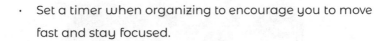

- Set a timer when organizing to encourage you to move fast and stay focused.

- Use stackable storage solutions in solid colors that have smaller containers inside. If you do use bins and baskets, label, label, label for the other "Clutterbugs" who may also be using your system.

- Place open baskets or bins on your desk or kitchen counter to hold your piles until you can get to them. This will be a visual reminder that your stack is getting too big for the basket and it is time to put it away.

- Make yourself a to-do reminder on your phone or computer that automatically reminds you of the tasks you want to complete each day.

- Turn off distractions like your phone, email, and television when starting a project.

- A labeler is your best friend. Label containers, file folders, and just about everything else to ensure that you (and your family members) put things away properly.

- Bento-box-style organizers are made just for you! Fill them with your smaller belongings and stack them..

- Embrace "good enough" organizing. Letting go of perfection can help you get so much more accomplished.

Photo Courtesy of Amy James, @OrganizedMomLife

I wish I had more words of wisdom for you other than to "do things a little crappier." In truth, you are just naturally a very organized person. The only thing standing in the way of a functional and clutter-free home is your drive for perfection. Once you can let go of the self-doubt and embrace your inner organizational superpowers, well, then I can start coming to *you* for organizing advice!

Cricket Testimonials

❝I can't thank you enough for helping me understand myself and my family, especially my hubby. I'm a Cricket and he is a Butterfly, so I was always frustrated with why he can't follow my system. Now you have helped me to understand his side and now I organize his stuff, his way. In common areas I'm flexible, and in my own spaces I'm completely myself and super organized. ❞

—Sonal, India

" I had to reach out and say thank you for the change in my home. I am a Cricket. I felt organized, but my house never looked organized. I had piles everywhere, which just seemed to go against my inner perfectionist. You showed me that my mess was *because* I was a perfectionist, not despite it. I've been macro-organizing and it's working. I know it's not forever and I will make it perfect when I have the time, but for now, the piles are gone and I feel really good about the way my home looks. "

—Emily, Ohio

" I never send emails like this, but here it goes. My wife made me take your test. I thought it was kind of BS, but when I read the descriptions, they hit the nail on the head. I'm a Cricket. My wife is a Butterfly. I was at my breaking point with her mess. I don't know why, but it just really resonated with me when I read that she just doesn't think like me. Anyway, we are working on making new places for her to put stuff. I took the closet doors off in our bedroom. I don't like it, but she is hanging up her clothes instead of leaving them on the floor. This is the first time in twenty-one years that I see real progress in our house. So, thanks Clutterbug girl. "

—Dave, USA

Chapter 10

Living or Working with
a Cricket

My Husband the Cricket

I've lived with a Cricket for almost seventeen years and, let me tell you, it's actually pretty awesome. For the most part, Crickets are tidy and pick up after themselves on a regular basis, which is a major bonus when sharing a space.

I've had so many people ask me, "How can I get my partner to pick up after himself?" and, while there are many strategies, I personally have never had to experience this struggle. Joe is much tidier and more organized than I am.

Crickets place an extremely high importance on putting things away properly, so the biggest issue isn't whether *they* are tidying their mess, but rather, whether everyone around them is.

Every morning, when Joe gets ready for work, he has to contend with the bathroom counter being strewn with my various products. I cannot get ready in the morning without completely trashing the bathroom, it just can't happen. I have gotten better at tidying it back up when I'm done, but the bathroom always looks like it's been ransacked while I get ready. Joe, on the other hand, puts each and every product immediately back when he is done using it. While you may think owning obnoxious amounts of bathroom products is a predominantly a women's affliction, I can assure you, my husband has a ridiculous amount of bathroom products too.

Photo Courtesy of Deborah Heritage

Crickets, regardless of gender, are meticulous in everything they do, and it can be intimidating. They get frustrated when others fail to meet their high expectations. As a result, tensions arise when they share space with other Clutterbugs.

My husband spent the first few years of our marriage frustrated with my messy tendencies. I was constantly losing my keys, misplacing important papers, and generally just being a disorganized mess. He tried in vain, many times, to teach me to use his paper filing system.

"How hard is it to put the paid Visa bill in the folder labeled 'Visa'?" he would snap as he rummaged through messy piles of papers shoved in the desk drawers, looking for the bill.

"Sorry, Joe," I'd apologize, for the hundredth time. He'd roll his eyes and sigh, as if implying that he thought I wasn't really sorry at all.

It wasn't that I deliberately wouldn't use the filing system he set up, it just didn't even cross my mind. I'd pay the bill and then move on to something else, rather than stopping to take the time to use his beloved, yet *super complex*, detailed system.

Once my husband *finally* understood my natural organizing style and how different it was from his (I made him take the

Clutterbug test and read about each different bug type), he was able to relax his expectations of me and, by extension, the expectations he put on himself. Understanding fosters tolerance. Now that we both understand the reasons behind our actions, we no longer have the resentment that comes from unmet expectations.

It isn't realistic for a Cricket to expect his family, roommates, or coworkers to maintain his level of detail and perfection. Therefore, compromise on his part is key.

It's much easier for a Cricket to simplify their system than it is for other Clutterbugs to try and force themselves to use a detailed one that works against their natural style.

If you live or work with a Cricket and feel pressured to meet their high expectations, or are embarrassed by failing to meet them, encourage him or her to read this book. Just by understanding the four organizing personality types, they will be much more likely to adapt and compromise on their ideals and expectations.

Piles for Miles

I'm not implying that living with a Cricket is always a cakewalk; they can definitely be messy as well. **Their need for visual simplicity is trumped by their need for perfection, so a Cricket is a classic piler.** They will pile things to put them away properly "later," but sometimes, that "later" never arrives.

My husband used to pile and, let me tell you, those piles were the bane of my existence. As with most Crickets, paper is the biggest issue because it takes constant diligent maintenance. The need for a really detailed organizing system means that Crickets prefer a filing system with an abundance of categories. A filing cabinet or file box is their paper organizing system of choice, but setting up a detailed filing system takes time. Even once a system is set up, maintaining a detailed paper system is also time-consuming. Sorting each bill, statement, or other piece of mail into sub-categories requires a dedicated chunk of time on a weekly basis. When the system is too complex, many Crickets procrastinate on using it until they have "more time."

This paper procrastination was the biggest issue that plagued my marriage for many, many years. When we first got married, Joe was the designated person to take care of paying our bills. He has always been much better at money management than I, so it made sense that this task would be his to look after. Every day, the incoming mail would be stacked on our tiny desk for Joe to pay the bills "later." He didn't want this pile of mail filed away, for fear of forgetting about it. He also didn't want to take the time to deal with it every night, right when he got home from work. You can probably imagine that, by end of the week, the mail pile would have grown so huge that the desk would be unusable. When I "cleaned," my Ladybug brain would insist that the pile be out of sight, so I'd hide it somewhere in the office.

Without the visual reminder, Joe would forget about that pile. A bill or two would be paid late or be missed altogether. My Cricket husband would be angry at me for hiding the pile and I would be angry at him for having a pile in the first place. It was a ridiculous game we played for far too long. It took us three years to attempt a different solution.

The first solution that we tried was having *me* pay the bills and sort the mail instead of him. I hated seeing clutter, so I would stash the mail in a basket and pay it once a week. Things would go downhill when it came to filing everything away after I had dealt with it. Joe had taken the time to set up an amazing filing system with categories for every piece of paper you could imagine. My Ladybug brain doesn't do sorted, detailed categories, so I shoved and hid those papers anywhere they would fit. When Joe needed one of the papers I had "filed," the hunt would be on. Tax time was a blur of frustrating hide-and-seek, lost papers, and an understandably angry Joe. It was an absolute nightmare. Worse, after the first go-round, we actually played this silly paper game for *another three years before we tried another approach.*

In the end, what worked for us was a combination of both our organizing styles. We opted for a file folder on the desk, clearly labeled "Incoming Mail" that Joe still drops the mail into and deals with on his own time. It is visual enough for him to remember, but hidden enough for me to leave it alone. Once Joe pays the bills and sorts the mail, he piles the papers into two macro categories, "Home" and "Business." I bought two large bins, each labeled with those same categories, and we now both have an easy place to put those papers until tax time.

It isn't an ideal Cricket system, that's for sure. If he needs to find something from one of the bins, it does require him to sift through to find what he is looking for. It's not ideal for my Ladybug brain either. I'd much rather have the mail sorting system off the desk entirely and both labeled bins hidden in the closet. But this is the art of compromise, and for us this system works well. We both know where everything is, nothing is ever misplaced, and we no longer fight over the piles.

Joe's Garage: A Slob Story

In our home, I've banished Joe's personal space to the garage. It's mean, I know (not to mention a bit of a stereotype), but with three kids in our fourteen-hundred-square-foot home, there just isn't another space that could be a dedicated Dad space. Besides, Joe loves woodworking, fixing, and general tinkering, so it makes sense that the garage would be his personal man cave.

Unfortunately for Joe, the garage isn't his *exclusively*. Our family uses the garage as an entrance way, along with storage for bikes, sporting equipment, and other garage-related goodies.

Poor Joe. The one space in our home where he can get his Cricket on is full of a lot of stuff that isn't even his.

I don't organize this space, which means I never tidy it either. It's his and his alone to manage. Yet, with so much stuff needing to find homes, just as with my other Cricket clients, it overwhelmed his perfectionist brain. "Where do I start? What is the best system? How do I organize all these categories properly?" While he tried to come up with a plan, the garage continued to fill up with more and more stuff.

Joe's biggest struggle in the garage was with his tools. He wanted them put away in a really detailed way so, in the meantime, he made lots of neat and tidy piles all over the garage floor. Eventually, there wasn't even any space to walk in the garage, and then his anxiety shifted to his tools getting lost or broken. On the one hand, he didn't want all his tools lying out, and on the other, he didn't want to put them away until he had the proper system designed.

And, just as with my other Cricket clients, this all too common paralysis requires a priority shift to overcome it.

For Joe, the transformation came when he finally let go of the overplanning and overthinking and decided to take action. He stopped procrastinating and dedicated an entire weekend to organizing the garage. To deal with the huge mess, he had to check his perfectionism at the door.

Our garage has a huge empty space above it, accessed by an old pull-down ladder. Joe's initial plan when we bought this house was to build new stairs to get up into a dream workshop with storage units for all his tools. Three years after we moved in, the space remained completely empty, and the bottom floor of the garage was a total disaster.

Joe had spent the intervening years researching the best tool chests and workshop organizing systems. If he couldn't find just the right one, he thought about building something himself. He had agonized over the best way to build the stairs, without taking away too much floor space in the garage. He planned and re-planned his dream workshop, wanting to ensure that everything was functional and properly organized.

Once Joe let go of his ideal vision for his fantasy workshop, he was able to embrace "good enough" organizing and began moving his tools up into the unfinished space. He started by macro-organizing (what a good student Joe was, he really did listen to me), placing power tools in one pile and hand tools in another. He put his vision of micro-organization on hold so he could at least get his tools sorted and put away, to start.

In just one weekend, Joe moved all his tools and supplies into the loft, and he now had his very own workshop. It wasn't perfect, and he still had to access it by pulling down that rickety old ladder, but it was a start. It was by lowering his expectations that he was able to stop the perfectionist procrastination and finally take action on creating his space.

After the initial macro-organizing session, Joe made taking action on his workshop a priority in his life. He scheduled at least one hour a week for setting up systems and creating micro-organized homes for tools and supplies. He meticulously sorted nails, screws, and bolts into bento-box-style organizers, and he even filed sandpaper in a paper filing system, sorted by the grade of the grit. He took the time to label every tiny drawer, jar, and compartment. In three months, his dream workshop was complete.

Joe's workshop is now the picture of Cricket organization. Everything is perfectly organized and contained in custom-built cabinetry. His work benches are completely clutter-free and, despite his doing woodworking on a regular basis, you'd be hard-pressed to find a speck of dust. It is by far the most organized space in our entire home, and Joe has no problem maintaining the detailed and meticulous organizing systems.

In the end, his workshop became everything that he had hoped it would be, but it required lowering his initial expectations to get there. This is the secret to helping Crickets overcome the indecision and procrastination that can come with perfectionism: embracing good-enough organization in the beginning.

A Cricket Plan of Action

When it comes to organizing or achieving any goal in life, it's important for a Cricket to first let go of the high expectations they put on themselves and begin with a simple, macro approach to planning.

Every Cricket is different, but if the Cricket in your life is really struggling with getting started, you can help them with the first two steps of Cricket organization, allowing them to do what they do best, which is step number three.

Step One—Macro Sort: When organizing a space, start by sorting items into large categories. If you are sorting tools, start by putting all the hand tools together in one pile and all the power tools together in another. Do not get distracted by sorting different types of screwdriver or categories of hand tool in the beginning; sorting into small categories and subcategories is always the last step.

Step Two—Find a Home: Once you have macro-sorted into large categories, decide where each category should belong. **For many Crickets, this step can also throw up a perfectionist roadblock.** Let's use tools as an example. Perhaps you decide that hand tools should go in a tool chest. Perhaps you can't find or afford the ideal tool chest at the time, so you might be tempted to wait until you find the perfect tool chest in the future. *Instead, embrace good-enough.* Use an old dresser, or even just an empty box if you have to; just ensure that everything has an organized home. Remember, you have the rest of your life to go back and make it perfect; this is about making it good enough today.

Step Three—Micro Sort: Once everything has been macro-sorted and has a dedicated home, it's time to get your Cricket groove on and create subcategories in a really detailed system. **Be sure to label everything as you go, as it's easy to forget where things are when you have a large number of subcategories.** This process is time-consuming, so be realistic in planning how much time it will take you to achieve the perfect system. I recommend scheduling yourself thirty minutes a week to dedicate to micro-organization. Let go of the desire to have it all done overnight to ensure that the process will be less overwhelming and you'll be less likely to get discouraged.

Compromising with a Cricket

The golden rule of combining styles is to default to the visual and the simple organizing solutions. Unfortunately for the Cricket, this means compromising both their need for visual simplicity and their desire for detailed organizing systems. *Sorry, Crickets.*

You can still have an organized and functional home, but expectations must be adapted for everyone to achieve success.

If a Cricket lives with a Bee or Butterfly, they must default to visual organization, which means open shelving, lots of hooks, labels, and clear containers to maintain organization long-term. Visual command centers with calendars, to-do lists, and mail sorting systems are a must. Hooks for coats, purses, and backpacks are much more realistic than expecting things to be stored behind closet doors. Daily-use items need to be easily accessible and visual, and the Cricket needs to have patience when encouraging their visual bugs to let go and purge unused items.

If a Cricket lives with a Ladybug or Butterfly, they must default to simple organization, which means fewer categories and more macro-organizing. You may need just one basket for paid bills and just one container for first-aid supplies, including everything from Band-Aids to pain relievers. Remember that using large, open containers is key to a Butterfly and Ladybug's success. They need to be able to toss items into the proper home without having to give sorting a second thought. While this approach may seem less organized than a Cricket would like, everything will have a designated home and can be put away easily, greatly reducing surface clutter.

With all this compromising coming from the Cricket, it's vital that they are given a personal space of their own to organize, just for *their* personal style. This could be a craft room, office, garage, or even just a closet of their very own. A

Cricket's need for detail and functionality is about more than just appearance, it's critical in helping ease their anxiety. A visually quiet and organized space both calms their soul and ensures that they always know where everything is. Order and structure are their happy place, so it's important that they have this in at least some areas of their home.

In a Cricket's own personal space, they need to be able to let their freak flag fly and get really detailed with their categories. Remember that setting up a Cricket system is a time-consuming process, so be patient while they make it happen. Micro-organization requires ten times the time and effort to set up, as well as much more effort and time to maintain. The plus side of a micro-organized system is that everything is much easier to find and a Cricket will have no problem maintaining it, once set up.

While it's vital that a Cricket default to macro-organization in shared spaces, it's equally important that a Cricket have spaces that exhibit their love of details and categories. They need to have their belongings organized in a really functional way, so make sure that some personal spaces can be dedicated just for that.

My last bit of advice for living or working with a Cricket is this: **don't move the piles.**

The worst thing you can do is move and hide the piles. The Cricket is probably going to forget about items that were in that pile, and it will only serve to justify their fear and increase their need to pile in the future. For better or worse, when in a hurry, that is the Cricket's go-to method. Although it may be hard for the rest of us to see it, either your Cricket sorted and organized those seemingly completely random piles the way they did for a reason, or at the very least, knows roughly where in each pile they will find something when they are looking for it. Ultimately, the piling comes from a fear of losing or misplacing physical things or outright forgetting something written on paper. They are afraid to forget about or lose items, or to make a mistake when organizing them. The piles are just their half-baked coping strategy.

So what can you do? Help your Cricket create "good enough" systems for those piles. Sometimes, it's just a simple basket that can contain the pile and act as a visual reminder to empty it when it's getting too full (think of the "homeless clutter" bins we use in my home, that I described in earlier chapters). At other times, new homes need to be created for items that have been piled, but be sure to be respectful when relocating these items and ALWAYS label the homes to help ease the Cricket's anxiety.

I may be biased, but the truth is, a Cricket personality makes for a wonderful roommate, partner, and coworker. A little communication and compromise can go a long way toward creating a space that works for everyone. Indeed, communication and compromise are key no matter what the combined Clutterbug styles may be.

Chapter 11

Leveling Up

Life Is (Kind of) Like a Video Game

On the track "Love the Way You Lie," Eminem says "Life is no Nintendo game," but I beg to differ. He's right in that we don't get to restart the game of life after falling off the edge, but we *do* need to beat each level before we get to move up to the next one.

Leveling up in life is a premise that I truly believe in. The concept is simple: We all want more from life. More time for the people we love and the hobbies we enjoy, more money in the bank, and more stuff that makes us happy. It's human nature to want to grow and be successful. Leveling up is an experiential process. **Before we can move on to bigger and better things, we first need to master what we currently have.**

In my life, I am always yearning for the *next step*. A bigger home, more time, and, of course, more money. I want to grow my business and expand my brand to include licensing and even franchising in the future. But I can't have *any* of the things I want from life if I don't streamline and master my business at its current size. How can I possibly take on more work when I can barely manage what I currently have?

So if you dream of having more time for the people and things you love, a bigger home for a bigger family, a nicer car, or more money in the bank, you must first be able to manage and maintain the house, car, and finances you have today like a boss.

Running Your Home Like a Boss

I left a career managing a non-profit to become a stay-at-home mom and, let me tell you, it was a rude awakening. I was a hot mess mommy. I was late for *everything*, I couldn't find *anything*, and I felt frantic and stressed-out all the time. How was it that I could manage a busy office and organization's programming in my career, but I couldn't seem to manage my own home?

The truth? I wasn't *trying* to run my home like a business, I was just trying to get through the day. In my career, I showered each morning, did my hair, and dressed in business attire as soon as I woke up. At home, I stayed in my pajamas all day long. In my career, I had a schedule and a list of important tasks that needed to be accomplished, with deadlines and expectations that held me accountable and motivated me to push myself to get things done. At home, well, I had no schedule and zero accountability, which resulted in little motivation. I played with my children and kept the house relatively clean but, other than that, there were no expectations to meet.

The day I decided to treat my home like a business and myself as the CEO was the day that everything changed.

I forced myself to get dressed each morning, which had a huge impact on my day. When I stayed in my pajamas, I felt tired and lethargic, no matter the time of day. When I got dressed, I felt more awake and energized. Incidentally, it also was nice to have pants on when unexpected company stopped by!

I created a simple daily schedule and put it on the fridge as a visual reminder of what was expected. Yeah, I had to force myself to adhere to it and it was hard at first, but I kept reminding myself to treat my job as a housewife like it was a paid position. **What would I expect from someone I was paying to look after my children and my home?** I asked myself this question daily and did my best to act accordingly. After a few weeks, my schedule was second nature and no longer a burden or chore to complete. Once I had mastered my daily schedule, I started adding in bigger tasks, like structured play and school time with the kids, and scheduled time to work on DIY projects around the house.

Eventually, my routines were simplified, and I found it easier to accomplish everything on my growing list. Despite doing more than ever, I felt like I had more free time than I'd ever had before. I had leveled up! I had mastered the stay-at-home mom thing, which meant I now had extra time in my day to add new things. It was then that I started Clutterbug.

Structure Is Freedom

Like many, maybe like you, I resisted structure for the longest time. To me, structure felt like conformity. I wanted my schedule to be free and open for anything that came along, so I had no schedule at all. I told myself I was "living in the moment" and that routines were rigid creativity killers. I had a lot of reasons for resisting structure, but I couldn't have been more wrong.

In the absence of a routine filled with positive, productive habits, I had unconsciously created a routine of negative, counterproductive, ineffective habits. Every day I would waste hours aimlessly browsing the internet or watching television, all the while feeling like I had no time for the things I really wanted to do. Without structure to my day, everything took longer to accomplish. I *felt* busy, but I wasn't *productive*. I wasn't accomplishing any of my goals or ambitions because I wasn't taking any positive action steps toward achieving them.

Setting and following schedules and to-do lists gave me more free time than ever before. I know, it sounds crazy and counterintuitive, but it's true! Whether you're a Bee, Butterfly, Cricket, or Ladybug, we all need daily structure and routine to make life easier.

So, now that you know your organizing style, it's time to start making real changes in your life. It's time to level up!

If you want to master your home, your finances, and your life, it all starts with a simple plan. Create a daily schedule of the basic tasks that you want to accomplish each day. Once you have mastered your daily schedule, to the point where it becomes an effortless habit, you too can start adding more goals to your daily, weekly, and monthly schedule.

Organization should be a goal for everyone, and you can start with a basic daily cleaning routine that includes a ten-minute tidy-up each day. Baby steps; you need to focus on the macro before the micro. So, once you have mastered this level of daily tidying, you can add in fifteen- to twenty-minute specific tasks, such as sorting your junk drawer or organizing your refrigerator. Remember to create new organizing systems that work with your Clutterbug style and each of your family members' styles as you go along. When you accomplish a new goal, however small, reward yourself for your awesomeness! Each small step you take will stack on top of the small step you took yesterday and, before you know it, you'll be leveling up on organization. Small successes gathered together over time add up to big change.

Mastering home organization is one of the greatest skills you can achieve. For a start, it's incredibly easy to accomplish and requires nothing more than consistency. Secondly, it's a gateway to so many other levels in your life. When you are in control of your home, you can't help but feel in control of your entire life. Being organized gives you access to more time, more money, and greatly reduces your stress. An organized home gives you a sense of calm and relaxation each night when you fall asleep and instills energy and motivation when you wake up.

For me, the change in my life was dramatic. I stopped feeling frantic. I had more time for my family and the hobbies that I love. I stopped re-buying things I already had, forgetting to pay bills, and wasting money on organizing systems that didn't work for me. I was able to start a business from home and actually have the space, time, and confidence to do it. Maybe it was my subconscious, the power of positive thought, or simply because I felt *in control* of my life for the first time. I really don't know. Heck, maybe it's a combination of all of the above. My point is, becoming the boss of your home gives you the ability to become the boss of your entire amazing life. I've heard stories from thousands of other families who have seen the same positive impact that comes from knowing your style and finally getting organized for good.

Today's the Day

Today is a blank page, my friend. It's the day to start to your new, organized life. Seize it, structure it, and get started right now. Write yourself a simple to-do list, create new daily schedules, and dive into organization with a new passion. Purge unused things, create new systems that work for your style, and label the heck out of every bin and basket in sight.

When you get discouraged, remember that the clutter that surrounds you did not accumulate in a day, so it won't be gone in a day either. Decluttering and organizing takes time. Don't despair: You're not only making your home more functional, you're learning a skill that's going to level you up in your life.

You may have days where you resort to old habits. That's okay. Try again tomorrow. I promise you, being consistent will get you to that clean and clutter-free home. As my experience has shown, creating new daily habits around your home will drastically improve every other area of your life as well. Now that you truly know yourself and your organizing style, you can stop setting up systems that will fail you and finally create the positive, lasting change that you have always known is possible.

Start small. The huge mess and task ahead of you is overwhelming. Take it one bite at a time. Focus on just one pile, one drawer, or one shelf, and when that's done, move on to the next one. Celebrate every victory. Each organized step on the road to Clutterbug Mastery deserves a little happy dance, because it's the small steps that create the big change that's coming.

Here are some simple steps to help you get off on the right foot:

Create a simple to-do list. Choose eight to ten small tasks that you want to accomplish. "Clean the garage" is too huge and overwhelming. "Declutter the shoes in the garage" feels and is much more doable, which makes it a great place to start.

Prioritize. After you have created your to-do list, mark it with three dots for the most important items, two dots for tasks of medium importance, and one dot for the tasks that have the least impact on your day (you'll find an example to-do list in this chapter). Always start with your highest-priority items. I call this approach to time management "Eating Your Frog," as it's based on the productivity book *Eat That Frog* by Brian Tracy. The method he creates, and names after this rather graphic metaphor, is simple: Tackle the most important and least appealing items on your list first, and it'll make the rest of your list seem easy in comparison. Brian Tracy named it after a quote he attributes to Mark Twain: "Eat a live frog first thing in the morning and nothing worse will happen to you the rest of the day."

Do each task until it's completed. I have ADHD, so I understand getting distracted easily. That is why it's so important that you create a list that only has small, easily attainable goals. It's equally important that you complete each task in its entirety before beginning another. Leaving a trail of half-finished projects will steal your mojo and get in the way of your progress. Nothing feels better than checking a completed task off your list. This warm, fuzzy feeling of accomplishment is what will motivate you to keep moving forward on your road to Clutterbug

Mastery. Take a moment to recognize and celebrate each of these little victories.

By knowing your style and following these three easy steps, you are going to be able to finally overcome the clutter once and for all.

Whether you are a Butterfly, Bee, Ladybug, or Cricket, these strategies will work. Following them faithfully will get you organized. It doesn't matter if you have been living in cluttered, messy squalor for decades and lost all hope of ever being able to change. Organization is possible for everyone.

Thank you for letting me be a small part of your journey. I'm so ecstatic that you have made it this far, and honored that you sought out my book for help. However, my inspirational attitude, personality insights, and practical tools can only get you so far. Now you have to take the tools you have learned, roll up your sleeves, and use them. Only you can make your goal of an organized, clutter-free home and less stressful life a reality. Believe it, my little Clutterbug, and your dreams will come true. You deserve it.

To Do List

Daily Planner

DATE:
_____

PRIORITIES:

1
2
3

WORKOUT:

WATER:
○ ○ ○ ○ ○ ○ ○ ○ ○ ○

MEALS:

B
L
D
S

MORNING:
_____
_____
_____
_____
_____

AFTERNOON:
_____
_____
_____
_____

EVENING:
_____
_____
_____
_____

NOTES:
_____
_____
_____
_____
_____

Today

SCHEDULE:

6 a.m. _____

7 _____

8 _____

9 _____

10 _____

11 _____

12 p.m. _____

1 _____

2 _____

3 _____

4 _____

5 _____

6 _____

7 _____

8 _____

9 _____

10 _____

DATE:

_____

AFTERNOON:

_____
_____
_____
_____
_____
_____
_____
_____
_____
_____
_____
_____

MUST DO!

_____
_____
_____
_____
_____
_____
_____

Acknowledgments

I am so incredibly thankful for everyone who has helped make this book possible.

My amazingly supportive husband, Joe: Your intellect and steady demeanor perfectly balance my full-blown crazy, and I'm so grateful for that. You continue to be my compass and I'm so lucky to be your partner on this ride called life.

My kids, Izzy, Abby and Milo: What the heck did I do without you? You give me more purpose and joy than I ever thought possible. Plus, you're all hilarious and my very best friends.

My publisher, Mango: I am beyond grateful that you took a chance on me. Working with you has been an incredible experience and I just can't thank you enough for all that you've done for me.

My editors, Hugo, MJ, Stephanie, Devin and Andrea: You guys rock! You helped me take my jumbled thoughts and make them clear and concise. All of you are so talented and I'm so grateful for your wisdom and expertise.

My assistant, Alysha: I am so lucky to have you! I learn something new from you every day. You bring some much needed focus to my business and I can't thank you enough for that. Don't forget about me when you're a famous filmmaker one day!

My amazing online community: I love you guys. A special thank you to those who have submitted photos for this book. Every single day I am moved and inspired by all of your support, encouragement, and the transformations that each of you has made in your lives. This book is for you and because of you.

About the Author

Cassandra Aarssen is the creator of the Clutterbug Philosophy, which helps people get organized by understanding their unique organizational style.

She has an engaged community, both in print and online, with two bestselling books and over half a million online followers. Her popular YouTube channel, blog, and podcast, *Clutterbug*, inspires and educates families with real life organizing ideas on a small budget.

Her new online course offers education and training as a Certified Organizational Specialist™.

When she isn't trying to rid the world of clutter, she's chilling with her awesome family in Windsor, Ontario, Canada.